The Life and Cuisine of

Elvis Presley

The Life and Cuisine of

Elvis Presley

David Adler

SMITH GRYPHON
PUBLISHERS

To Vanessa

First published in paperback in Great Britain in 1995 by
SMITH GRYPHON LIMITED
Swallow House, 11-21 Northdown Street
London N1 9BN

First published by Crown Trade Paperbacks in the USA in 1993.

ISBN 1 85685 098 6

Book design by Kay Schukhart
Printed in Great Britain by Redwood Books, Trowbridge

Acknowledgments

Thanks to:
Pauline Nicholson, Elvis' cook;
Billy Stanley, Elvis' valet and stepbrother;
Mrs. Marion J. Cocke, Elvis' nurse;
In Tupelo, Miss Vertie, who fed both Gladys & Elvis; Rev. & Mrs. Frank Smith,
Elvis' minister and his wife; Roy Turner;
In Hollywood, Barbara Eden; George Christy;
In Vegas, Lloyd Wentzell, Food and Beverage Director, the Aladdin Hotel and Casino;
the Las Vegas Hilton;
In the army, The Quartermaster Corps; Ann Harrison, Fort Lee Public Affairs
Specialist; Dr. S. Anders, quartermaster historian; the Pentagon;
At High School, Shirley Watkins, director of Nutrition Services, Memphis Public
School System.

Sharon Squibb, Angela Miller, Peggy Tagliarino, Kay Schuckhart.

Tim Ryerson, P.G. Auwaerter, M.D., Martha Babcock, Jeff Golenberg, The Gridiron
Restaurant, Coletta's Italian Restaurant, Phyllis McCabe and Hands Ink, Hilton
Hawaiian Village Hotel, Krispy Kreme Doughnuts, and Continental Bakeries.

My testers, Jean Galton and Paula Disbrowe; and my taster, Daniel Barr, whose
waistline expanded with each recipe.

INTRODUCTION 8

1 A TASTE OF TUPELO.............................11

2 SCHOOL DAYS.....................................25

3 1950S ROADSIDE CUISINE 33

4 THE ARMY MESS.................................43

5 THE GRACELAND MEALS.......................65

6 ELVIS' SNACKS 91

e n t s

7 ROOM SERVICE WITH ELVIS' VALET 101

8 ELVIS EATS IN HOLLYWOOD......................109

9 VEGAS CUISINE.....................................123

10 LOVE ME SLENDER: THE ELVIS DIETS 133

11 THE TRAGIC DINNERS 139

12 THE LAST SUPPER 147

EPILOGUE: ELVIS LIVES? 151

PHOTOGRAPHY CREDITS 155

INDEX 156

I n t r o d u c t i o n

Tell me what thou eatest,
and I will tell thee what
thou art.

—Brillat-Savarin

Elvis' valet, Billy Stanley, told me that when Elvis ate, he would "race through the rabbit food [salad] real fast so he could get to the real stuff." That's what I was in search of, "the real stuff" that Elvis devoured: buttery biscuits, a six-egg western omelet served with a pound of burned bacon, a case of Eskimo Pies, and of course, the fabulous "Fool's Gold Loaf." All were foods fit for the King.

Unlike most celebrities who are distant from their fans, Elvis was a star of the people; Elvis, rich and famous, was still one of them. His cuisine reflects his life— both innocent and fabulous, and in the end, possibly just too much. Food, his first love, was the love that destroyed him.

Given the vast sweep of the King's life, we owe his menus and favorite dishes to the American popular cuisines he became immersed in during the various stages in his career. Although rarely explored in traditional cookbooks, this is the real food of America's greatest star, and of America itself—Vegas food, high school cafeteria food, army food, Hawaiian cuisine, "white trash" Southern country food, packaged foods, teen food, and the celebrity food of Hollywood.

But Elvis cuisine is also distinctly Elvis. Elvis did everything his way, and this holds true for what he ate. Despite its popular origins, his is fantasy cuisine, food eaten without fiscal limitation or physical inhibition. Elvis cuisine is Southern food raised to baroque new heights. It's snacking without guilt. It's scoring an entire vending machine's worth of junk food. Elvis cuisine is literally food lust. As someone who knew Elvis well disclosed to me, and as I will discuss later, Elvis even used food in his sex life.

I hoped my investigation would yield a new portrait of Elvis and his world, and a particularly insightful one, given that nothing was more important to Elvis than his Menu. My search for the holy grail—to eat exactly what Elvis ate (and get the recipes)—led me into the King's world. In Tupelo, Mississippi, I attended a family reunion at the Elvis Presley birthplace featuring local foods, and I met the woman who fed Elvis' mother scraps from her table, keeping her from starving. I spoke to the wife of Elvis' minister about the church picnics ("dinner on the ground") that were a favorite of the young Elvis. To gain insight into Elvis' army years, I attended the U.S. Army Cook School at Fort Lee, in Virginia.

My quest also led me to the opulent buffets of Vegas, to the spectacular luaus of Hawaii, and to the glitz of Hollywood dining where I discussed what Elvis ate with his old friend, "I Dream of Jeannie" star Barbara Eden.

Memphis, of course, was where I conducted most of my research. I interviewed the head of the Memphis schools' cafeterias, had breakfast, lunch, and dinner at Elvis' favorite restaurants, and shared a pizza with Elvis' valet, who knew all the secrets. I interviewed Elvis' nurse, who tenderly fed him her special banana pudding at the end. It was when I had dinner at Elvis' cook's house (chicken fried steak, mashed potatoes, and crowder peas), cooked in pots once owned by Priscilla and served on plates from Graceland, that I almost felt like a guest at the King's own table.

The recipes I collected are important for multiple reasons. First, they are interesting sociological artifacts, evocative of another era. Second, there is something to tempt every palate, from the simple to the perverse; and most of the recipes—chicken fried steak, corn bread, and banana pudding come to mind—are genuinely succulent. Third, and most important, Elvis ate them. If he *is* still alive, this book might just appeal to him more than any other.

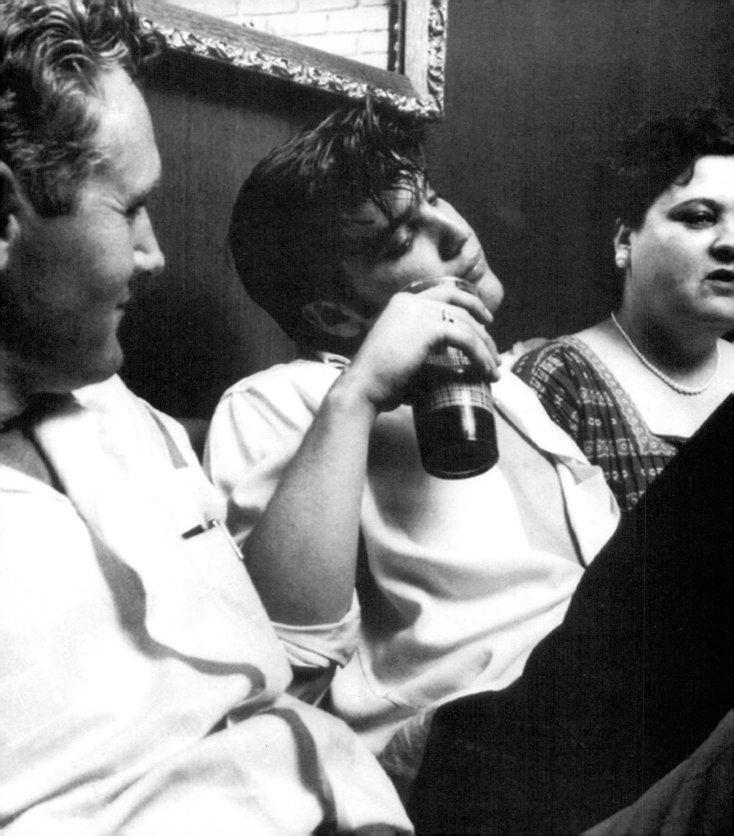

ladys Presley's pregnancy was difficult. She was carrying twins, and she had a bad liver. Even so, she had tried to keep working at a shirt factory. But though the job paid seventy-five cents a day, money that she and her husband, Vernon, desperately needed, she was too ill to keep working. Gladys took to her bed to await the birth of the twins.

The habit then, in Tupelo, Mississippi, during the 1930s was to pass around the hat when a fellow worker's baby was going to be born. The women at Gladys' factory, concerned about her health, raised nearly ten dollars, a huge sum at a time when a twenty-five-pound sack of flour cost only seventy-five cents. In most cases, the money would be given to the family. In this instance, the

feeling at the factory was that they had better not give the Presleys the money "'cause Vernon would drink it up." The women instead used the money to buy sheets and blankets for the babies.

Miss Horton, the factory manager, lent her car to Miss Vertice ("Vertie") Quigley, Gladys' closest friend at the factory, to carry out the gifts. The Presleys lived in the poorest section of Tupelo in what is known as a "shotgun shack." You could shoot straight from the front door through the front room, the back room, and out the back door, and hit every room along the way. In fact, the two-room shack with its neatly swept dirt yard was so small that it was closer to a manger than a full-sized house.

Miss Vertie drove out to the Presleys', carrying the gifts for the twins. As soon as she entered the house, she knew something was wrong. In the tiny front room she came across an eerie scene. Placed on the center table, a table not much larger

than a lampstand, was a white box covered with a sheet. She pulled back the sheet to find that the box was a coffin. Inside was a little dead baby. It was the dead twin, Jessie.

Gladys lay on her iron bed close to death. When she saw Miss Vertie she began to cry. She cried because her baby had died, because she was so sick, because the women at the factory had given her gifts. Miss Vertie left "as quick as she could." Though Miss Vertie couldn't see him, in the back room a baby cried with Gladys. It was the surviving twin, Elvis.

Gladys, probably still hemorrhaging, was taken to the hospital in Tupelo. Elvis was carried to the hospital, too, though he was by all accounts fine. He was taken with his mother solely for the purpose of being nursed. It was Elvis' primal eating experience. In the face of death, for Elvis, food and life and love were one and the same.

Tupelo, Mississippi, is located in the hill country close to Tennessee. It therefore lies at the junction of two Southern regions: the coastal, or plantation, South and the highland, or hillbilly, South.

The Oxford and Brandeis historian David Hackett Fischer has identified distinct food traditions associated with each region. During the seventeenth century, the coastal South, unlike the rest of America, was known for its feasts, which "could be staged on short notice or no notice at all." A French traveler arriving unexpectedly at a plantation found that he was treated "'royally, there were all kinds of beverages, so there was a great deal of carousing.'" The feast, which included roast beef, puddings, and pies, sounds remarkably like one at Graceland three hundred years later.

In contrast, in the Appalachian South, Fischer found the "foodways" were primitive and casual. Families survived on pork (boiled or fried), which was rarely eaten elsewhere in the colonies, and a "truck patch" of greens. "The 'standard' supper dish in the mid-eighteenth century was a wooden bowl of milk and mush." This resembles Elvis' standard supper at the end of his life.

These two violently contrasting food traditions obviously affected the adult Elvis' diet. Together with the drama of his birth, they helped make Elvis cuisine the most fabulous food story of the Twentieth Century.

The poor in Tupelo during the 1930s all ate the same food: corn bread, a mess of greens, fried okra, and, if you had the money, a piece of meat. If everyone generally ate the same food, we know exactly what the Presleys and their baby ate. We know because Aunt Lillian, Gladys' sister, told Gladys' biographer, Elaine Dundee, and the historian Roy Turner. The Presleys ate what Aunt Lillian grew. She had a vegetable garden, what she called a "truck patch." Aunt Lillian gave any excess produce to the new family. In the spring she offered them mustard greens; in the summer peas and butter beans, okra, eggplant, and tomatoes; and in the fall turnip greens and collard greens. Vegetables popular in the North, like carrots, celery, and lettuce, were not part of the picture.

Using Aunt Lillian's ingredients, Gladys prepared her favorite "victuals" for her child and her husband. But Gladys was never really domestic. Her goal in life was always to be a movie star. However, her love for her newborn baby was so intense that she miraculously turned herself into a cook, expressing her love for Elvis through food.

Gladys, like any Southern cook worth her salt, never used recipes. She selected proportions and seasoning according to tradition and taste. Therefore, we can only reconstruct her cooking style and specialties. If we are to do it in the most historically accurate way, we must first examine her culinary inspirations.

Her mother, Doll, was certainly not such a source. Doll was a bedridden invalid and had little time to teach Gladys about the finer points of culinary artistry. Aunt Lillian taught Gladys much more about domestic routines. Another possible source of inspiration for what Gladys knew about proper Southern cooking and what to feed Elvis was the same Miss Vertie who brought her the gifts when Elvis was born. Miss Vertie's father was the owner of a prosperous country store. It was Miss Vertie who had fed the young and hungry Gladys, the child of dirt-poor tenant farmers across the road.

Miss Vertie still resides outside Tupelo, having outlived both Gladys and Elvis. I visited her at her house in the country, which is larger than most and has a front porch running its entire length. Though quite ancient, Miss Vertie is still sharp and peppery. Remembering Gladys and her siblings, she says, "They were naked and nasty children. My daddy wouldn't let people like that come to the table. I fed them scraps from the kitchen." Though Miss Vertie isn't sentimental about it, those scraps given to what she refers to as those "snotty-nosed children with dirty hair" kept them alive. Gladys later told Miss Vertie's mother that if it weren't for this food, she "would have starved to death."

Miss Vertie knew Elvis, too. She used to drive him in to Tupelo to perform on the show of local radio star Mississippi Slim. After one show, she told Elvis that while she was busy in town, because it was raining, he could wait for her in her car.

Miss Vertie, at her house outside Tupelo.

When she got back to her car, he wasn't there. As soon as she started it up, Elvis popped out from behind a tree, drenched. Despite the rain, he had been too shy to get in her car without her. And he was so shy that he never said a word on the entire trip back.

It is clear from this story that Miss Vertie had some affection for Elvis. This isn't true of her friend who is visiting in Miss Vertie's parlor during our interview, the even more genteel Miss Nessie Chesnut, who frowns. She is not impressed by Elvis: "He was nothing but hillbilly trash. Only a hillbilly would carry a damn guitar."

I interrupt to ask Miss Vertie if I can take her picture, as she is one of the origins of Elvis cuisine. "Certainly not," she snaps. "I'm old and I'm ugly. I used to be young and ugly but now I'm old and uglier—five feet ten and only a hundred pounds." I tell Miss Vertie that she isn't ugly (and she isn't). We decide that she will be photographed wearing her trademark—a sunhat from her extensive collection.

As she puts on her shoes to walk out to the porch, she agrees to the picture only on the condition that I don't use her real name—"There are too many Presleys in the neighborhood and too many fans." I agree to the condition. Miss Vertie is not her real name but one I have chosen. Miss Chesnut suggests that I call Miss Vertie a different name, which makes Miss Vertie laugh: a UFO "because she's flown through life."

Miss Vertie told me how she made the Southern staples that kept Gladys alive, forming the inspiration for what Gladys served Elvis. They are, in their own way, the family heirlooms of Elvis cuisine.

Miss Vertie told me how she fixed these dishes. All recipes have been developed and adapted from Miss Vertie's verbal directions.

Miss Vertie's Corn Bread

1¼ cups all-purpose flour
¾ cup white cornmeal
2 teaspoons baking powder
¼ cup sugar
½ teaspoon salt
1 cup buttermilk
1 large egg, slightly beaten
¼ cup melted lard

Preheat the oven to 425° F. Grease a heavy skillet with additional lard. In a large bowl mix the flour, cornmeal, baking powder, sugar, and salt. Stir together the buttermilk, egg, and melted lard. Stir the wet ingredients into the dry just until combined. Place the skillet over a medium-high heat for 2 minutes or until hot. Pour the corn bread batter into the skillet and place in the oven. Bake 15 to 18 minutes or until a cake tester inserted in the middle comes out clean.

Yield: **1 skilletful**

Miss Vertie's Greens

Gladys would serve mustard greens in the spring when they ripened in Aunt Lillian's truck patch. To cook these bitter greens, you must first rip off the leaves and wash and wash and wash. When you think you're done, you must wash some more. Turnip greens, eaten by the Presleys in the fall, are sweet. Collard greens, another fall crop, have the most pronounced flavor of all and are slightly bitter. They are the favorite green of black Southerners. Aunt Lillian grew them and the Presleys ate them. Greens in Tupelo are always served with pepper sauce, often stored in an old Coca-Cola bottle.

1 piece fatback
1 bunch greens
Pepper Sauce (recipe follows)

Boil the chunk of fatback in a cast-iron pot in water to cover. Add the greens—collard, turnip, or mustard. Boil till tender. Serve with Pepper Sauce. (To be authentic leave in the fat. During the Depression, even if you weren't as poor as the Presleys were, you would have eaten it.)

Yield: **4 servings**

Pepper Sauce Hot Enough to Send a UFO Flying

Hot peppers
Vinegar

Pick hot peppers, pour vinegar over them. Store in an old Coca-Cola bottle for several months until vinegar is hot.

Elvis, of course, didn't eat this grown-up food when he was an infant. As soon as Elvis was old enough to eat solid food, Gladys adapted these recipes to a baby's needs. Gladys fed Elvis a special nursery food, the one most common in poor homes of the region. It was called "goody mush." "Goody" was the slang word for the highly prized inside of the corn bread. To make the "goody mush" Gladys crumbled the goody into a mashed vegetable such as peas, forming a porridge for her son. This was Elvis' first "solid" food.

Goody Mush

Canned peas
Corn Bread (see recipe, page 15)

Cook the peas and mash them, then crumble in the corn bread. Serve while still warm. Elvis was not fed out of a silver spoon.

Gladys also had another favorite baby food for Elvis. It was called "soaks."

Of all of baby Elvis' nursery foods, the

"Soaks" (For Baby Elvis)

Corn bread
1 glass buttermilk

Dunk the corn bread in the buttermilk.

It's a satisfying snack, even for an adult. It's easy to see why Elvis returned to "soaks" in later life, eating them in bed at Graceland.

one he lived for (and on) was peanut butter on crackers. Elvis' personality shows through in his voraciousness for these crackers. As soon as he could walk, "he could eat his weight in peanut butter and crackers," according to Elvis' uncle Vester, Vernon's brother. Uncle Vester used to tease Elvis by telling him that he was going to eat up all the peanut butter and crackers before Elvis could get to them. Elvis would become hysterical. At the mere sight of Uncle Vester he would scream to his mother, "Hide them, Uncle Vester is going to steal them." And if she didn't, Elvis would pull up a chair to the counter and hide them himself.

Young Elvis, fussed over by his mother, was content with this basic diet of bread, lard, peanut butter, and greens. There was only one thing missing: meat. Because Elvis never had steak, he never missed it; steak just wasn't eaten in the homes of poor people like the Presleys. Even Miss Vertie, despite her generosity to Elvis' mother, never gave Gladys valuable food like beef, which she kept in an icebox with the Coca-Cola.

But though there certainly was no beef on the Presleys' table, meat did make an occasional appearance. The Presleys were country people. They could live off the land. Nothing was more mouthwatering to Elvis than the sight of his father returning home with a shotgun in one hand and a freshly shot squirrel in the other. Gladys cooked squirrels with dumplings—just like chicken—or fried them. We offer you the fried version using a recipe popular in northeastern Mississippi during Elvis' time.

Fried Squirrel

To cook a squirrel, first go out and try to kill a very young one. This is the most important thing as old ones are too tough. When skinning the squirrel, make extra sure to remove all the hairs.

2 young squirrels, skinned and cleaned
Salt to taste
¼ teaspoon freshly ground pepper
4 tablespoons butter
½ cup all-purpose flour

After carefully washing the squirrels, pat dry. With a mallet, gently pound the meat until the bones are crushed and the flesh is tender. Season the meat with salt and pepper. Melt the butter in a skillet (preferably cast-iron) over medium-low heat. Dredge the meat in the flour, and add to the melted butter. Brown and turn. Continue cooking, stirring occasionally, until the meat is golden brown and cooked through. (Pierce with a knife to check doneness. The juices should run clear when cooked.) The process should take 25 to 30 minutes.

Yield: **Enough for a small starving family**

Fried potatoes go well with squirrel, but fried tomatoes are even better.

Fried Green Tomatoes (Mississippi style)

4 large green tomatoes
⅓ cup vegetable oil
Salt and freshly ground pepper to taste
¾ cup all-purpose flour

Soak the tomatoes for 20 minutes in ice water until ready to use. Slice the tomatoes about ¼ inch thick. Heat the oil in a skillet over medium heat. Mix the tomatoes with the seasonings, and dredge them in the flour. Fry the tomatoes in the hot oil until golden brown. Serve hot, or at room temperature.

Yield: 4 generous servings

Squirrel was indeed a special treat. But more commonly, the meat found in the Presley household was "streak of lean." This is a type of fatty bacon that Gladys used for seasoning. On weekends, after Vernon got his paycheck from his job at the laundry, he would on occasion bring home not just the bacon but the family favorite—pork chops. They were battered and fried in a skillet until black. Elvis' cousin, Corinne Tate, says that though she doesn't know about the "high-priced stuff when Elvis got older that rich fellows ate," when he was in Tupelo, pork chops were his favorite food.

The beverage of choice during these happy childhood meals was iced tea, served the only way it's made in the South—extra sweet. Coffee, which became so important to Elvis later, was drunk only by the rich or professional classes.

Elvis, well fed and lovingly cared for by his parents, was on his way to a happy childhood. However, these early blissful eating experiences for Elvis came to an abrupt end when his father was arrested for forging a check for the sale of a pig. Vernon was sent to Parchman Penitentiary. The effect on Elvis' diet was dramatic. Gladys and Elvis, who was only three, had to go on "relief." Their "welfare commodities," as they called them, consisted of butter, lard, flour, grits, and cheese. Gladys prepared grits with the cheese, making what is the true Southern subsistence dish, one usually considered too grim or desperate to find its way into cookbooks. Little Elvis ate them in order to stay alive. Grits weren't as popular in Tupelo back then as they are now, but Gladys had to use them. Even if your daddy isn't in the penitentiary, you might want to try these. Not only will they ease your hunger, but they are surprisingly delicate.

Grits and Cheese

4 cups water
1 teaspoon salt
1 cup grits
6 tablespoons margarine
8 ounces Velveeta cheese
2 eggs
Evaporated milk (see approximate amount below)
Dash cayenne pepper

Preheat the oven to 325°F. Bring the salted water to a boil in a large saucepan. Stir in the grits and bring back to boil. Adjust heat to low, and cover, simmering for about 17 minutes, or until the grits are thickened. Stir occasionally. Melt the margarine and the Velveeta together and mix into cooked grits. Lightly beat the eggs in a 1-cup measuring cup, and finish filling the cup with evaporated milk. Fold the egg mixture and the cayenne into the grits. Pour the grits mixture into a greased 2-quart casserole. Bake until lightly brown, about 25 minutes.

Yield: **Easily feeds a family of 6**

Elvis' father didn't come home from prison for three years. Those were desperate times for Elvis and his mother. They had only each other for support. Facing starvation, they survived for weeks on end on only grits and cheese, supplemented by vegetables from Aunt Lillian's garden. Mother and son became closer than ever. They developed a pri-vate language. Gladys was called "Satnin'," feet were "sooties," and milk was "butch." The two also shared a bed. What little money Gladys had she spent on expensive toys for Elvis. But despite their intimacy, relying only on each other wasn't enough. Gladys and Elvis needed help, more than the welfare office could provide. They found it, both spiritually and gastronomically, in the Lord.

The First Assembly of God

The First Assembly of God is a fundamentalist sect that believes in the reality of the supernatural. According to the church, the Holy Spirit is among us. So is the Devil. Services are "physically agitated"—the preacher and the congregation jump and twist in the aisles, leaping to outsmart the Devil. Perhaps all this movement is why the establishment in Tupelo calls the First Assembly of God by its better-known name: Holy Rollers.

Elvis and Gladys, who had sampled many churches, at last found salvation at the First Assembly of God. As Elvis sat with his mother, members "testified" about anything "unusual" that had happened that week, be it the work of God or the Devil. The Devil could be anywhere. Members swayed their bodies and raised their hands to the Lord to ward off Satan. Little Elvis and the rest of the congregation sang hymns of praise, interspersed with darker tales of the supernatural. The testifying and prayers grew more intense. At their most ecstat-

ic, people spoke in tongues and literally rolled in the aisles. Gladys rocked Elvis, their hands clapping on the off beat, as shouts of "Praise the Lord!" filled the air.

Dinner on the Ground

Following this ecstatic release, the congregation silently filed outside for "dinner on the ground," the country phrase for a type of church picnic. This Bible Belt brunch was served at lunchtime after the singing but prior to the sermon. The picnic was an integral part of churchgoing; the service on the whole was referred to as "singing and dinner on the ground." The food was particularly important to Elvis and his mother because of their poverty; in fact, most of the congregation wasn't much better off.

The women of the church spread out sheets on the ground (hence the picnic's name) and then laid out copious portions of the delicious fare they had brought from home—fried chicken, which kept well without refrigeration, biscuits, congealed salads, and—what Elvis liked best of all—a vast array of heavenly desserts.

The congregation circled the sheet to choose their favorites. They then went to eat leaning against their cars, parked under the shade of giant trees. They sipped iced tea and lemonade. Elvis rested in the shade with his mother.

Dinner on the Ground (on a table).

Emotionally spent from all the singing in the church, Elvis was absolutely silent as he concentrated on eating.

To make your own dinner on the ground, you'll need a white sheet, a grassy knoll with shade nearby, and the Tupelo specialties featured on the next page.

Elvis' father was released from prison in 1941 when Elvis was nearly six. Vernon moved his family to Pascagoula, Mississippi, where he found work in a shipyard. But Gladys was unhappy with the Gulf town. "We're not staying down there," she said, "watching all those uptown folks eating shrimps and oyster." The family returned to Tupelo.

Back in Tupelo, Elvis came under the influence of the country singer Mississippi Slim. Elvis accompanied him each Saturday morning to WELO, the local radio station where Slim broadcast his show "Singin' and Pickin' Hillbilly." Elvis was entranced as he watched him perform.

Elvis' best friend during this time was Mississippi Slim's younger brother, James Ausborn. James remembers that as a child Elvis spoke a lot about hamburgers. There weren't that many places to get hamburgers in Tupelo at that time. One of the cheapest was Dudie's Diner, which served a hamburger reputed to be made with bread or canned salmon as filler. Dudie's was all that Elvis could afford. He would save up his money for the hamburger. It was a good walk to the diner, close to three miles, but Elvis and James undertook it anyway. As he ate the burger (with mayo) and drank an RC, Elvis talked about how good it all was, how it was the grandest thing in the whole wide world.

Oven-Fried Chicken with Potato Chips

1 fryer chicken, cut into 8 pieces
Freshly ground pepper
½ cup margarine
2 cups crushed potato chips

Preheat the oven to 350° F. Wash and dry the chicken, and season with pepper.
Melt the margarine in a skillet and cool. Roll the chicken pieces in the melted margarine, and then roll them in the
crushed chips. Place the coated chicken parts in a greased, shallow baking pan, and bake in the oven 50 to 60
minutes, depending on the size of the chicken. (Check the poultry after 30 minutes of baking. If the coating is
browning too quickly, make a loose foil tent over the pan.)

Yield: 4 servings

Bible Belt Brunch

7-Up Salad

1 package lemon gelatin
1 package lime gelatin
2 cups hot 7-Up
1 cup cottage cheese
1 can crushed pineapple
Green food coloring (if desired)

Prepare gelatin according to the package directions, substituting 7-Up for water. Let cool to room temperature. Stir in the remaining ingredients. Pour into pretty individual salad molds or mold as desired. Let set in refrigerator for several hours. Tupelo tip for unmolding: Dip the chilled mold in warm water for a second before serving.

Chess Pie

This magnificent Southern delicacy is really a sugar pie. According to legend it received its name when someone asked, "What's for dessert?" and a modest cook replied, "'Jes pie."

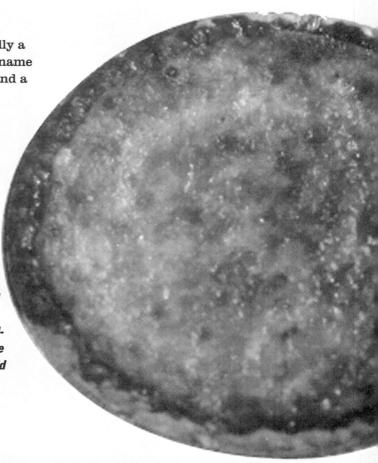

½ cup butter
3 cups granulated sugar
2 tablespoons flour
4 large eggs, beaten well
1 cup whole milk
¾ teaspoon vanilla extract
2 9-or 10-inch unbaked pie shells

Preheat the oven to 325°F. Cream the butter and sugar together until light and fluffy. Add the flour and beat a few seconds more. Add the beaten eggs, the milk, and the vanilla. Pour into the unbaked pie shells and bake until the filling is firm, approximately 1 hour. When done, the top should be brown and crusty, and batter should not coat a silver knife inserted into the center. Cool completely before cutting.

Yield: 2 pies

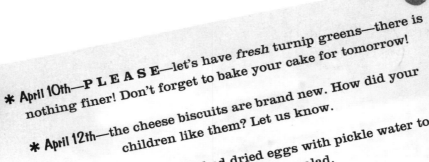

* April 10th—**P L E A S E**—let's have fresh turnip greens—there is nothing finer! Don't forget to bake your cake for tomorrow!

* April 12th—the cheese biscuits are brand new. How did your children like them? Let us know.

* April 13th—Use hard-cooked dried eggs with pickle water to make a delicious potato salad.

* April 15th—Bologna Cup: Leave outside skin on bologna; fill with whipped potatoes, top with cheese. Heat in oven until cheese is melted and bologna has curled.

* April 28th—Make a peach roll like a jelly roll. Use plenty of spice, lemon, and honey and make the pastry rich. Use a peach butter sauce to have a dessert they will never forget!

Memphis City School Cafeteria Worksheet, 1950

Monday
Glorified Hot Dogs
Hash Brown Potatoes
Cole Slaw
Baked Apple with Whipped Milk
Topping
Milk

Tuesday
Chicken Pot Pie
Spinach
Grapefruit and Orange Salad
Biscuits—Butter
Chocolate Pie—Milk

Wednesday
Shepherd's Pie with Potato Topping
Turnip Greens—Cole Slaw
Corn Bread—Butter
Cranberry Betty
Milk

Thursday
Italian Spaghetti
Green Beans
Spiced Beets
Fruit Jell-O Salad
Plain Muffins—Butter
Ice Cream—Milk

Friday
Fish Flake Salad
Bean Soup
Cabbage—Carrot Strips
Buttered Toast Strips
Fudge Cake—Milk

TENNESSEE STATE DEPARTMENT OF
EDUCATION SCHOOL LUNCH PROGRAM
MEMPHIS CITY SCHOOLS
MARCH 1952

Bus drivers, MBAs, airplane pilots, baggage handlers, screenwriters, beauticians, veterinarians, plumbers—no matter what they're doing now, every American has once eaten in a high school cafeteria. The food has indelibly marked our palates. The mere mention of school cafeterias conjures up memories of mystery meat, soggy fish sticks waiting on the steam table, and mashed potatoes ladled out with an ice cream dipper by a grouchy cafeteria worker wearing a hairnet. The social ambience was equally unpleasant: students screaming and yelling, the clatter of plates, the slow food lines, the linoleum floors and fluorescent lights, the smell of ammonia and spilled milk, the jock in the corner stealing someone's milk money. Most of us hated the food. Elvis didn't.

After his father moved his family from Tupelo to Memphis, Elvis attended L. C. Humes High School, at 659 Manassas, and graduated in 1953. No one remembers Elvis's initial reaction to his high school food because, the truth is—for his first years at least—no one remembers him at all. During his freshman year at Humes, Elvis was just another social nonentity in overalls fresh out of Mississippi, stunned by his arrival in the big city. To make matters worse, his mother used to walk him to school and back each day.

But Elvis changed. Though he continued to let Gladys walk him to school, he experimented with his hair. He first tried a mohawk before he hit upon the classic duck's ass created for him not by an ordinary barber but by a beautician. Good-bye to the overalls. In their place he sported two-toned western shirts and fancy pegged pants bought at a ghetto store. A classmate remembers that, as a final touch, Elvis "often tied a red bandanna around his neck" in the fashion popular with interstate truck drivers of the era.

The effect at school was immediate. His classmates tried to beat him up. But everyone noticed him as he strutted in, his hair heavily brilliantined, to take his place in the cafeteria line, and sample from the banks of steam tables the school dietitians' best efforts.

Elvis' high school menu, shown here (opposite), is archetypal American public school cafeteria. It recalls a bygone era when high school still held out the promise of self-improvement, lessons in citizenship, an innocent teen culture, and a job after graduation.

Elvis didn't look at it this way. He wasn't concerned with self-improvement. He just liked the lunches at Humes' cafeteria—extra peanut butter sandwiches were always available for seconds. There was just one problem. He usually wasn't

A Memphis high school cafeteria, 1950.

Mrs. Shirley Watkins, director of Nutrition Services for the Memphis school system.

out the other usher. The job ended. What would he do now?

At Humes High, Elvis' shop teacher noticed that Elvis lingered after class. Shop was the last period before lunch hour. Realizing that Elvis was skipping lunch, the teacher asked Elvis what was wrong. Elvis told him he didn't have the money for lunch. The shop teacher gave him lunch money that day and for many days afterward. Elvis became a shop major.

When Elvis did eat lunch, he sampled more cosmopolitan menus than the Southern foods he was raised on. Though the Memphis schools' cafeterias served foods all the students were familiar with—such as corn bread and biscuits—they also served exotic fare like Sloppy Joes or "Italian spaghetti." Elvis was from rural Mississippi and had never been exposed to foreign food before. When he tried it, he liked it; Italian food became one of Elvis' favorite cuisines for the rest of his life. For Elvis, unlike anyone else, high school cafeteria food was a broadening experience.

He was lucky, too, that he was going to school in Memphis, where the schools were concerned with their students' tastes and welfare, as the worksheets indicate. Even cafeteria officials at the archrival Shelby County School District admit that Memphis Nutrition Services run a "first-class operation." The goal in the 1950s was not just to make food that was as good as any other high school's. The cafeterias had more ambitious plans. As the April 1950 worksheet proudly noted, the school's Texas Salad ("a fancy congealed salad plate") compared with "anything downtown."

The person currently responsible for

there. And this wasn't because he wasn't hungry. The fact is, more often than not, Elvis couldn't afford lunch.

Elvis' father later said, "There were times when I never had more than twenty-five cents to give Elvis for lunch money, but he never fussed about it." And Elvis was lucky if he even got that much. His solution was to get himself a job as an usher at the Loews State Theater. To his delight, the girl at the candy counter used to sneak him candy. Another usher reported him, and when Elvis found out that he had been snitched on, he punched the food of the Memphis public schools is Shirley Watkins, director of Nutrition Services. Her office in the school system's administration building is clearly identifiable by the framed jigsaw puzzles of food outside. Shirley is quite a sophisticated woman. When she reads the worksheets and menus from Elvis' day, she is tickled by their naïveté and innocence. At the same time, she takes her job today of feeding 106,000 schoolchildren with appropriate seriousness. "Our commitment to nutrition and health is for real," says Shirley, who is so nutritionally correct that no frying is allowed in the schools. "Even what we call 'fried chicken' is really made by baking chicken."

Shirley explains why Italian food in the Memphis schools, both in Elvis' day and now, has not ventured beyond the spaghetti-with-meatballs stage. When she put manicotti on the menu, "It was not that well received." She dryly notes, "We love Italian in Memphis but we're not that Italian."

If Elvis had been able to eat more at Humes' he might have been a more successful athlete. More than anything, Elvis wanted to be a football player. He tried out, and went to a few practices. But he was cut from the team. In his friend Red West's judgment, "With a bit more weight...he just might have made a good guard, but things didn't seem to work out."

Though we all remember high school food, we've never known how to make it. Here's how. All recipes are for foods served to Elvis, from the Memphis public schools, March 1951.

Memphis Schools' Grape-Nuts Flakes Cookies

1 pound plus 9 ounces oleo
3 pounds plus 7 ounces brown sugar
1 can dry eggs (or egg substitute)
2½ pounds all-purpose flour
¾ ounce baking powder
½ ounce salt
¼ ounce cinnamon
1 pint water
1¼ cups milk
1 pound Grape-Nuts Flakes
2½ pounds raisins

Preheat the oven to 425° F. Cream the shortening with the sugar. Add the eggs. Sift the dry ingredients; add alternately with the liquid. Add the Grape-Nuts Flakes and raisins last.

Drop on greased baking sheets. Cook in hot oven 10 to 12 minutes.

Yield: 14 dozen
Recipe Source: Memphis Public Schools

Butter Cookies

Anyone who attended Memphis schools in the 1950s remembers these delicious cookies. They were a luxurious treat, and Elvis, like everybody else, looked forward to them after lunch. Sadly, because of budgetary cutbacks, these buttery cookies are no longer served in the Memphis schools.

7 pounds butter, USDA
2 quarts plus 1 cup granulated sugar
4 tablespoons plus 2½ teaspoons vanilla extract
8 pounds all-purpose flour, USDA

Preheat the oven to 400°F. Cream the butter and sugar until light and fluffy. Add the vanilla and the flour. Mix well. Drop with a number 40 scoop on baking sheets and flatten with a fork. Bake for 10 to 12 minutes.

Yield: **320 servings** Serving Size: **1 cookie**
Recipe Source: **Memphis Public Schools**

Memphis School cafeteria workers, 1950s.

Sloppy Joes

Memphis schools were equally beloved for their Sloppy Joes. Sloppy Joes are still part of the school system's menu.

1 cup water to rehydrate onion flakes
¼ cup dehydrated onion flakes
18 pounds ground beef
5 tablespoons granulated sugar
6 tablespoons prepared mustard
2 quarts plus 2 cups tomato ketchup
5 tablespoons salt
100 hamburger buns

Add water to onion flakes and let stand for 20 minutes. Drain. Sauté onions until clear but not brown in a small amount of oil. Brown the ground beef, draining or dipping off excess fat as it accumulates. Add the onions and remaining ingredients. Simmer 20 minutes to allow seasoning to be absorbed. The mixture should be moist but hold its shape when placed on a bun. Place approximately 3 ounces of the meat mixture on each bun.

Yield: 100 sandwiches
Additional Information (per school recipe file): To prevent the buns from becoming soggy, sandwiches should be made up on the serving line. They should not be prepared ahead of time.

Cheese Spoon Bread

6 cups powdered milk
6 quarts plus 3 cups water
4 cups yellow cornmeal
4 tablespoons salt
6 tablespoons butter
6 cups grated Velveeta cheese
3 cups dry eggs

Preheat the oven to 350°F. Mix the powdered milk and six quarts of the water. Scald 4½ quarts of the reconstituted milk in a double boiler. Blend the cornmeal with the remaining 1½ quarts of milk and gradually stir into the hot milk. Cook until smooth and thickened, stirring occasionally. Add the salt, butter, and grated cheese, stirring to blend. Mix the dry eggs with the remaining water. Slowly pour the hot mixture over the well-beaten eggs, stirring constantly. Pour into a well-greased baking dish. Bake in a moderate oven for about 1 hour, or until browned.

Yield: 48 servings

If you're making this for an adult instead of for a schoolchild, cheese spoon bread is enjoyable as a party savory, like cheese straws.

3 1950s **R o a d s i d e   C u i s i n e**

a n d
O t h e r   T e e n
T e m p t a t i o n s
f o r   E l v i s

Rock and roll was the heartbeat of teenage culture in the 1950s. Cruising the strip in finned cars was the spirit. Fast food consumed in finned cars was the soul.

Teen culture in the United States in the 1950s was something fundamentally new. Teenagers have always been around, of course. But for the first time in history, amidst the general affluence of postwar America, something new emerged: a separate culture for teenagers, with its own icons, consumer traditions, and foods.

For American teenagers, with their drag races, drive-ins, and disposable culture, the emphasis was on informality and fun. In this sense, teenage culture was the pacesetter, the leading edge of the new style of postwar America. The country was engaged in a consumerist frenzy, and fantasy and energy marked the look of American consumer goods. Drive-in hamburger stands looked like spaceships, cars resembled airplanes, and the old-style heavy jukebox was replaced by the mini, one to each booth at a diner.

Just as in 1950s design, where the frankly fake was favored over the real, in 1950s food, manufactured simulations replaced traditional ingredients in recipes whenever possible. This was the era of "Mock Apple Pie" made with Ritz Crackers instead of apples. Best of all, the directions were right on the back of the box. More often than cookbooks, the "back of the box" provided many recipes of the era. Any artificial snack made from a prepackaged mix was considered more modern than an elaborate sit-down meal made from ingredients found in nature.

If most 1950s food in general looked unnatural, the food of the strip—of drive-ins and diners—looked radioactive. Oversized burgers sprouted out from under their buns; luridly colored cakes wore shocking pink icing; root beer floats frothed strangely. All hinted of exposure to "the bomb." And atomic imagery was popular in the restaurants themselves. Lamp fixtures were shaped like rockets, while tables and curtains were decorated with satellites and atoms.

The design critic Thomas Hine has

Chocolate pie at the Gridiron, Elvis' favorite diner.

coined the term "populuxe" to describe the general look (including that of food) and the attitude of the postwar era. He calls it a time of "optimism and opulence," of "innocent hedonism." For Hine, "the populuxe era began with Elvis Presley—sexy, energetic, American." Elvis was even in tune with the atomic themes of the era. He was billed as "The Nation's First Atomic-Powered Singer."

Elvis may evoke this era of uninhibited consumption, but during most of his teen years he missed out on it. Elvis arrived at his prom in a decade-old Lincoln. His date was the fourteen-year-old Regis Vaughn, who sported a strapless pink taffeta dress. The young couple entered through a heart-shaped door at the Peabody Hotel to find the band playing and couples dancing cheek to cheek. Regis was excited at the thought of dancing with Elvis, until he informed her he "didn't know how to dance." Instead they spent the evening in the corner sipping Cokes.

Following his graduation from high school, Elvis didn't have the time, money, or wheels to participate in the flashy 1950s teen culture of the strip. He was too busy working—as a truck driver. He had landed a job at Crown Electric. His days were spent delivering wire. Nights were spent touring the little towns of the mid-South. He would often appear with the gospel group the Blackwood Brothers, a Coca-Cola always in his hand. There was little time to sleep—or eat. As Elvis' friend Red West later remembered, "We didn't miss many meals, but we sure postponed a darned lot."

Elvis ate in a hand-to-mouth manner or off the hospitality of fellow musicians. Not quite a freeloader, he was nonetheless excited about any invitation that came his way. While touring, Elvis once met June Carter, a singer later married to Johnny Cash. She told him to drop by if he was ever in Nashville. When he went there one weekend in 1955, he was flat broke and hungry. Elvis immediately went to June's house. She wasn't home, but this didn't stop Elvis. He took her at her word to make himself at home—and so he broke in.

Inside he found a spectacular kitchen hung with shiny skillets. Elvis pulled some off the wall and handed them to sidekick Red West, who set to work frying up some bacon and eggs. Oddly, as the eggs became harder, the pans became softer. Eventually, they completely melted into the burners. Elvis and Red ate bellyfulls of the eggs anyway, and then, "like a couple of bears," fell asleep. Elvis awakened to find a shotgun pointed at his nose. June's husband was furious, and not only at the break-in. Someone had ruined his wife's collection of antique copper pans, which were for decorative purposes only. But when he realized the perpetrator of the crime was Elvis, he laughed, and invited Elvis for a second breakfast.

Soon Elvis no longer had to break into houses in order to eat. He could sing for his dinner. Once he hit his stride, his rise to the top was meteoric. He was the nation's most famous teen, the King of Rock and Roll. He was denounced by the Reverend Billy Graham and caused riots when he appeared in New York. Elvis was a fantasy teen. And Elvis could now have a teen fantasy life.

The first thing he needed for this new life-style was his own car. The car he bought might have been used, but it was the best car there was: a Cadillac. Unfortunately, the "Cad" exploded and burned on a trip to Texarkana. But with the insurance money, Elvis bought a new Cadillac. He had this one painted in his favorite colors—pink and black. For the first time Elvis was ready to live teenage life as it is lived only in the movies. Cruising in the Cad through Memphis, here's what he stopped to eat.

Fried Dill Pickles

Elvis came across these pickles at roadhouses outside Memphis; fried pickles are the perfect accompaniment to beer. They are believed to have been invented at the Hollywood, a roadhouse originally in Hollywood, Mississippi.

8 dill pickles
½ cup flour
¼ cup beer
1¼ tablespoons paprika
1¼ tablespoons cayenne pepper
1¼ tablespoons black pepper
½ teaspoon salt
2 teaspoons garlic salt
3 dashes Tabasco

Cut the dill pickles in slices as thick as a silver dollar. Mix together the remaining ingredients to form the batter. Dip the pickle slices in batter and quickly fry in grease at 375°F. until pickles float to the top, in about 4 minutes.

Liberty Land Fairgrounds

Cotton candy, hot dogs, caramel popcorn—all favorites of Elvis—were the foods of the fairgrounds in Memphis. Once he became a rich teen, Elvis would rent out the fairgrounds, known as Liberty Land Amusement Park, for himself and his friends, closing the park to the public after midnight. Elvis and his entourage rode all the rides—the Whip, the Tumblebug, the Rocket, and Liberty Land's roller coaster, called the Pipin. The concessions were left open for Elvis. Before a trip on the Pipin, he always made sure to polish off a candy apple or some cotton candy.

He once invited a fourteen-year-old guest, Becky Yancey, to ride the Pipin with him. She had already spent too much time at the concession stand and was feeling queasy, but a request from Elvis was a command performance. As the roller coaster plunged down from the highest peak, she opened her mouth to scream...but vomited instead, all over the King.

The Memphian Theater

Following his entertaining pattern, the teen (and later the adult) Elvis had private midnight screenings at the Memphian Theater. They were attended by about one hundred of his friends. Admission was free and so was the popcorn, but you had to watch the movie on Elvis' terms. Elvis made the projectionist repeat his favorite scenes. If the action got slow, such as during a love scene, the projectionist would have to skip to the next good part. Elvis once saw *Dr. Strangelove* three times straight, with a number of scenes repeated so he could figure out exactly what was going on.

Elvis liked James Bond and *Patton* and any movie with Peter Sellers. His favorite movie of all time was Sellers' *The Party*. It's about an Indian movie extra who is accidentally put on a Hollywood party list and wrecks all the parties he's invited to. Elvis thought *The Party* was hilarious. He saw it again and again.

At the movies, Elvis always had a tray of candy set up next to him. His valet (his stepbrother Billy Stanley) arranged the candy for him. The valet knew exactly what Elvis wanted, and he would pay for it—he carried Elvis' briefcase. The King, like the British Royal Family, never carried money. As Elvis said: "I don't have to go out and buy things, I got Billy here to go out and buy them for me."

Elvis' Movie Snack

Here's what Elvis' valet always put on Elvis' tray at the movies.

Reese's Peanut Butter Cups
Jujubes
Peanut brittle
Bit-o-Honeys
A big ole thing of Pepsi

Mix up all the candy on a tray and place next to you at the movies. It should be too much to fit into a bowl. Wash down with Pepsi.

If Elvis was "into" the movie, then he wouldn't eat. If it was a boring movie, then he'd eat a lot.

The Gridiron

While cruising along the strip in his Cadillac, it was the neon-lit drive-ins and diners, with their new disposable "fast food," that caught Elvis' eye. He and his date would head to the Four Flames, a restaurant near downtown, for malteds or Cokes. The owner would never allow Elvis to pay. Elvis always left her a tip, which he would usually hide in the phone book. She would open it to find one hundred dollars. By that point, Elvis was already on his way to his date's house.

When Elvis moved down to south Memphis, the Gridiron became Elvis' favorite roadside restaurant hangout. It is still open, at 4101 Elvis Presley Boulevard (Route 51). With its polished shiny grill, long lunch counter with small round stools, and vinyl booths in the back, it is a classic example of 1950s restaurant architecture. Elvis never sat at the counter on the streamlined backless stools; he always took a table by the window or one of the large booths.

The food at the Gridiron matches its fabulous fifties interior. There are classic malt shop items: fries, pies, floats, and burgers; something for every hungry teenager. Elvis and his entourage of buddies, known locally as the Memphis

Mafia, would arrive in the Cadillac. Often one of Elvis' dates would come in tow, specially dolled up for the occasion. One attraction of the Gridiron was that it was open all night. But the main reason Elvis went there was because the Gridiron was the home of his all-time favorite hamburger, the "Palm Beach Burger."

Hungry boy that he was, Elvis always washed down his burger with a thick chocolate shake. At the Gridiron, after they fill your glass, they also set down on the counter the metal beaker the shake was mixed in because they make more than can be poured into one serving. The metal beaker is beaded with condensation from the cold. Elvis loved it that as soon as he finished one glass of shake, he could pour in more. As you pour out the shake the last drops are mostly chocolate syrup. This was Elvis' favorite part.

Elvis' Favorite Hamburger: "The Palm Beach Burger"

You can see why Elvis' burger deserves its glamorous name simply from reading its description on the Gridiron's menu: "Grilled choice beefsteak served with aromatic and sweet, gently melted pimento cheese, crisp lettuce, mayonnaise, and pickle rings."

1 hamburger patty
Hamburger bun
1 tablespoon pimento cheese
Mayonnaise
Lettuce
Pickle slices

Put the hamburger patty and the bun on the grill. When you are ready to turn the hamburger, take the top of the bun off the grill and spread it with a level tablespoon of pimento cheese. Then set it on the hamburger and let the pimento cheese melt over the meat while it finishes cooking. Meanwhile, take the bottom of the bun and spread it with mayonnaise, add a thin layer of lettuce, and several slices of pickles. When the hamburger is done and the cheese is melted, put the two halves together and serve on a small plate.

Recipe Source: **the Gridiron Restaurant**

Chocolate Shake à la Gridiron (for Elvis)

3 small scoops vanilla ice cream
6 ounces hot milk
2 ounces chocolate syrup

Put the ice cream into a milk shake can. Add the milk and the syrup. Mix on a shake machine until the ice cream is mixed in and is no longer in lumps. To remove the can from the machine, push it up. This cuts the machine off. Then bring it straight down, so the mixer won't splatter any out of the can. Pour the shake into a tea glass, and serve it with a straw. Set the can on the counter so the customer can finish up what's left in it.

Recipe Source: **the Gridiron Restaurant**

Sometimes Elvis would instead drink a Coca-Cola Float.

Coca-Cola Float

Coca-Cola
3 scoops vanilla ice cream

Fill a beaker with Coca-Cola. Add three scoops of vanilla ice cream. Mix well to get that spectacular fizz.

Recipe Source: **the Gridiron Restaurant**

The food and setting are but one part of the roadside restaurant ambience. The other ingredient is the human side of the story—the waitresses. What would a 1950s diner meal have been for Elvis without a gum-snapping waitress, her hair teased into a beehive with a little cardboard cap? Under her pink uniform, she was probably tougher than her truck driver customers. At the Gridiron today, the waitresses wear a red Scotch plaid uniform. They are much more hospitable than typical roadside waitresses, maybe because it's the South, or maybe because they're nicer to begin with. Even so, the Gridiron has strict rules for behavior.

The waitress who most frequently waited on Elvis at the Gridiron was Ann Lyon. She couldn't be more professional or more polite. She remembers Elvis coming in with his friends and taking a booth in the back. At the Gridiron, he didn't hide his tips. He always left them for Ann tucked under the edge of his plate.

When Elvis got older, he became too famous to go out in public, and Ann no longer saw him at the Gridiron. Late one night in the 1970s a man appeared in old overalls. He asked for several Palm Beach Burgers to go. Ann recognized her old customer at once—it was Elvis! He had slipped out of Graceland in a disguise so he could get his favorite burger.

Gridiron Do's and Don'ts for Service

✓ Do wear a hair net.

✓ Don't chew gum.

✓ Do wear hose.

✓ Don't wear excessive makeup such as eye shadow. This is only for going out in the evening.

✓ Do wear a whole slip if necessary so no one can see through your uniform.

✓ Don't tell a customer your troubles.

✓ And finally, "a customer is not someone to argue or match wits with."

Source—**Gridiron employees' manual**

Mom

Elvis, America's most rebellious teenager, relished roadside teen cuisine, but it was to his mother's kitchen that he always returned. No one ever said no to Elvis, or told him to eat up his spinach, least of all Gladys. The unique food bond between Elvis and his mother, forged in his infancy, flourished when he became a teenage rock star. When he left the projects and bought the ranch house on Audubon Drive, one of his first acquisitions was a Mixmaster—actually two of them—bought before he purchased the washer or dryer. Elvis told the clerk at the hardware store, "I want my mama to have two Mixmasters, so we can put them at each end of the kitchen counter and it'll cut down on the walking she has to do."

Elvis placed Mom's food even ahead of his career. One of his first newspaper interviews ever was with Martha Babcock, a cub reporter on the *Memphis Press Scimitar*, who had received an assignment to check out this unknown teen singer and find out why all the young girls were so crazy about him. Martha usually traveled with a photographer, but her editor considered this story to be so insignificant that none was assigned.

Martha arrived at Elvis' house on Audubon Drive to find it surrounded by twenty screaming girls. She entered by the side and was met by a maid wearing a starched white uniform. The maid led her through a room filled nearly to the ceiling with fan mail and into a room in the back where she told Martha to "set" down and wait. Down the center hall, Martha spotted a pair of skinny legs sprouting from a rocking chair. The legs were wearing clunky brown men's shoes. It was Elvis' granny, "Dodger."

Martha continued to wait. Vernon and Gladys tried to distract Martha from the fact that Elvis was late. What made the situation most irksome to Martha was that until her assignment, she had never even heard of Elvis. And now he was nowhere to be seen, even though she was from a newspaper. Where exactly was Elvis?

"Elvis is having his dinner," the maid told Martha, using the old-fashioned phrase for "lunch." And from the other side of the door to the dining room, Martha could make out the grunting sounds of someone eating. "I want some of that gravy. Give me some of that light bread" (the Southern term for Wonder Bread and others like it). Martha thought to herself that Elvis didn't like to chew. Evidently, nothing, not even the chance for one of his first newspaper interviews ever, was going to keep Elvis from his dinner.

And then the grunting stopped and the door to the dining room opened. Elvis came and stood in the doorway, and flexed his arms above his head. He was wearing tight black pants and a black silk shirt unbuttoned to the waist. Gladys, pretty and plump in a tent dress, beamed at her son. Elvis smiled back sleepily. It was clear to the young reporter that what mattered most to Elvis wasn't the interview, but Mom's food.

Sometimes Gladys made Elvis hearty dinners like the one Martha overheard being eaten. More typically she made him one special snack, which Elvis liked to eat and Gladys lived to make: fried peanut butter and banana sandwiches. Elvis had them for breakfast, brunch, dinner, and lunch, as well as for a midnight snack.

It was a teenager's dream, to eat only what he wanted, and there was no curfew either. Establishing the pattern he kept for the rest of his life, Elvis gave up the constricting convention of regular meals. That was what celebrityhood meant. It also helped to have a mother like Gladys, who was more than happy to make her son's fantasies come true. It seemed as if Elvis would never have to eat like a regular mortal again. Once, for seven weeks, Elvis lived only on peanut butter and banana sandwiches.

Fried Peanut Butter and Banana Sandwich (as recollected by Billy Stanley)

2 slices white bread
2 heaping tablespoons smooth peanut butter
½ very ripe banana, mashed with fork
2 tablespoons margarine

Spread the bread with the peanut butter and the banana. Melt the butter in a skillet over medium heat. Fry the sandwich, browning it on both sides. Serve warm. Use a knife and fork to eat.

4 The 🐟 Army Mess

A VISIT TO THE ARMY COOK SCHOOL

We're soldiers first, and cooks second," Sergeant Smale of the U.S. Army Cook School barked at me. I believed him. He looked very fierce, though no fiercer than a cook at a formal restaurant, which in fact was his occupation before joining the Army. (He worked at the Four Seasons in New York.)

I was visiting the cook school, at Fort Lee in Virginia, as part of my research on army cuisine. I had arrived at the fort earlier in the day. Fort Lee itself is a horseshoe-shaped complex, filled with low-rise wooden barracks dating from World War II as well as more modern pre-fabs. Fort Lee is the home of the army's quartermaster corps, the corps that feeds, clothes, and buries soldiers. The corps, "a cradle-to-grave operation," oversees the cook school. After I drove through the low-security front gate I first went to meet Ann Harrison, the public affairs officer who was to escort me on my visit.

The fort's publicity office is housed in a modern, trailerlike building. The clerks behind the information desk were munching on doughnuts. Out bustled Ann, who turned out to be a jolly civilian, a person who clearly made the correct choice in becoming a publicist. After warning her staff of the health hazards of doughnuts, Ann turned to me and said,

"So you're here to see the Ninety-four B's?" I had no idea what she was talking about. "Ninety-four B's stands for Ninety-four Bravo. Army terminology for a cook." Once we cleared up my confusion, Ann led me out the back door to her car. Before we got out, Ann asked me if I was superstitious. "Why?" I asked, wondering if there was some curse associated with the fort. "Because we're going out a different door than you came in," she explained, referring to a Southern superstition I had never before encountered.

I safely made it to her car. We first went to visit the quartermaster historian, Dr. Anders. I wanted to ask him about the army chow of the 1950s that Elvis Presley would have eaten. A military band marched outside the window of Dr. Anders' office, which was filled with filing cabinets and looked like an office belonging to any academic. But Dr. Anders, who is a Vietnam vet, has the short haircut and taut physique of a military man. At the same time, he has an intellectual air, befitting his Ph.D. in history. Because he is a quartermaster historian, his work encompasses both food and death.

Delicious and so nutritious.

He interrupted his research on techniques of handling a body after chemical warfare (apparently a brief internment is the easiest way to decontaminate a corpse) to speak to me about what Elvis ate. Rations were the focus of Dr. Anders' food research, and he began by defining for me what exactly a ration is: one day's feeding in the field. Dr. Anders told me Elvis' rations were a variation of the C (for combat) rations developed for World War II. Elvis' ration consisted of "a meat product, fruit, crackers, and a can opener." As this was field food, it was designed to be eaten either hot or cold. Dr. Anders didn't know which way Elvis preferred to eat the ration.

Elvis' garrison food, the food in mess halls, was stodgy and fried, according to Dr. Anders. Like rations, it too had a World War II flavor to it, cooked from recipes that hadn't varied much since that time. Modern mess food has changed drastically since Elvis' day and is significantly lighter. In fact, messes are no longer called messes but are now known as dining facilities.

I asked Dr. Anders why army food, which in every other sense is so rationalized and regulated, has such a decidedly Southern flavor (which is one reason why it made Elvis feel at home). The meat is usually the flesh of the hog, and it always seems to be fried. He explained that the food reflected the preponderance of army bases in the South. (Most army bases seem even to be named after Southern generals. I was at Fort Lee; I've never heard of a Fort Grant. It's almost as if the South had won the war.) The army favored the Southern locale because the warm climate meant more training days.

During lunch at the officers' club (a chef's salad) Dr. Anders and I discussed dissimilarities between the Gulf War and the Vietnam War. Afterward, Ann Harrison picked me up to take me to the cook school. She was happily eating a fast-food burger in the car. Only troops in basic are forced to eat in messes—or, rather, "dining facilities." Before we got to the school, I asked Ann how she would describe army food. "It's just like Morrison's," said Ann. Ann was referring to a cafeteria chain in Richmond. As I was to see, good army food resembles good cafeteria food—decent, plain, ample, and cheap.

There are forty-one thousand cooks in the army. It is at Fort Lee that Sergeant Smale and others on the staff of the "Army Center for Excellence, Subsistence" teach them how to do their job. The cook school itself is housed in a building that looks like a modern high school, except that the students lounging outside were all in camouflage.

They attend the school for an eight-week program. Cooks who successfully pass are assigned to messes around the world, but return for advanced training. (I never found out what happened to those who fail.) The school building is also home to the army's home economists, who make daily menu decisions for army messes around the world, involving eight hundred thousand meals.

When I arrived, Sergeant Smale directed me to the small-quantity cooking class, the first course for all budding army chefs, taken right after basic training. Before I left for class, Sergeant Smale gave me his favorite army recipe, for SOS, short for Shit on a Shingle.

Students in the small-quantity cook-

Me with Sergeant Smale and students at the U.S. Army Cook School.

ing course were preparing tomato soup for four when I visited. Sergeant Moses, the instructor, taught the basics of food preparation, such as the difference between baking ("to cook by dry heat") and boiling ("to cook in liquid at boiling point"). The soup was an easy dish, but that was the point; the four-person serving size made any mistake less catastrophic than if the students were preparing a batch for one hundred. Unlike advanced chefs, no one was cooking by instinct. Instead, everyone was carefully measuring proportions, even for water in the soup. This was exactly as it was supposed to be. All recipes were uniform, what the army calls its "standard product." Sergeant Moses taught his students twenty-three "products" a week—for dishes such as tomato soup, buttered broccoli, and meat loaf. Sanitation was emphasized. CLEAN AS YOU GO and SAFETY FIRST were

written on the wall.

I left for baking class before the soup was finished, so I don't know how it came out—though I'm sure it was sanitary. That day's baking lesson was butter cookies. Ann Harrison accompanied me to the course. A school official dressed in fatigues showed us the way. Though I didn't know this officer, I was curious if he cooked for his wife at home. "My wife's from 'Nam, Dave," he replied, "so she insists on doing all the cooking."

In the baking class, Sergeant Rea's students were cutting cookie dough using a special curved knife. In order to get cookies of the regulated thickness, they used a ruler to measure each slice. The students were inexpert at the job. Rulers shook, knives fell, and the slices came out more "homemade" than was hoped for. Nonetheless, the students, in their aprons and white hats and closely cropped hair, earnestly tried again and again. Like many army recruits, they came from modest backgrounds. It seemed strange to find a roomful of adult soldiers unselfconsciously measuring cookie dough.

Sergeant Rea's curriculum also included more advanced baking projects. I was surprised at how the army encouraged decoration. Sergeant Rea taught students how to decorate apple pies with pastry butterflies and flowers. The day I was there, however, he concentrated on portions. The cookie recipe (for one hundred) could be reduced to cookies for twenty-five merely by dividing by four. Sergeant Rea also focused on baking time, which, of course, is as important as thickness in influencing a cookie's chewability. The standard army recipe calls for a slightly crispy cookie. The students and I gathered anxiously around the industrial oven to await the results of our well-intentioned efforts. Sergeant Rea was not completely pleased with the results—the cookies were not crisp enough. But though the students looked downcast, Ann and I were rapturous as we bit into the first batch of gooey and thoroughly enjoyable U.S. Army butter cookies.

BASIC TRAINING AND BEYOND

An army marches on its stomach.
—Napoleon

Elvis Presley became Private Presley when he was drafted. US53310761, as the King was known to the army, reported for induction at Memphis' Kennedy Veterans Hospital on March 24, 1958. Elvis viewed going into the army with dread. "It's like starting all over again," he said gloomily. "It's like when I was working at Crown Electric. Seventy-eight dollars a month." His fans were equally

U.S. Army Cook School students.

disturbed, to the point of being uncontrollable; awaiting his arrival, they surrounded the brick induction center. Elvis' black Cadillac limousine slowly made its way through the frenzied mob. Elvis stepped out sporting polished motorcycle boots, his final flourish as a civilian.

Following his medical examination (which he passed), Elvis was immediately bused out to Fort Chaffee, Arkansas. A swarm of fans pursued him; his bus was able to leave Memphis only through the intervention of the military police.

The army tried to feed the King en route to Fort Chaffee. The attempt ended in disaster. Elvis's military bus was scheduled to stop at a diner called the Coffee Cup in Arkansas. Two hundred fans had gotten advance word and had infested the roadside restaurant. Elvis was unable to get off the bus. In the end, the bus driver went in and brought Elvis a paltry sandwich.

Elvis, who habitually slumbered into midday, began his first day at Fort Chaffee with a start. Reveille got him up at dawn. The army informed him that he would soon be marched off to have all his hair chopped off by a military barber. Like a condemned prisoner, he was allowed a meal—in this case, breakfast—before the fateful hour.

Elvis sulkily entered the mess for his first taste of army chow. Scores of photographers descended upon him to record what was to become a national publicity event. He sullenly made his way down the food line, filling his tray as he went. The food was served to him army style, in compartments rather than on plates. This clearly was going to be an army breakfast rather than an Elvis breakfast. Gladys would have made him whatever he wanted, even if it was just a peanut butter and banana sandwich.

Ignoring the photographers, Elvis carried his tray of chow back to his seat and dropped it with a smack on the table. He looked at the fried eggs and sausage that comprised this first army meal (the army keeps records of its menus dating back to World War I). Refusing to smile for the cameras, the King tasted his breakfast, which glistened from the grease it was fried in. Elvis was surprised and reassured. It was the best thing about the day. Army cuisine, by definition the most all-American of cuisines, was going to suit Elvis just fine. The army was to be a two-year nightmare for Elvis, but army chow was far from the living hell he had imagined.

Army food was intentionally reassuring. The army understood the importance of food to morale. The postwar army technical manual TM 10-405, *The Army Cook,* advises: "Well-cooked food is one of the chief means of keeping men contented and alert under the pressure of Army life." It ominously warns that if the chow is bad, "the disgruntled soldier [can become] a menace to his unit."

In the past, the army paid less attention to its cuisine. In the Spanish-American War, two-thirds of all deaths occurred in the continental United States, at Tampa, Florida, or other domestic bases. The ravages of battle didn't cause the deaths. Contaminated food from bad canning and poor latrine placement were responsible for the casualties. Army cooks at this time were untrained and simply distributed the food in the field. Alarmed by the death toll in the war, Congress intervened and mandated the revamping of army chow, putting it on a more regulated footing.

By Elvis' day, at the height of the cold war, the preparation of army chow resembled a precise military operation. Messes could only use authorized recipes, and each recipe was always for one hundred servings. The Army Subsistence Research Center in Chicago scientifically developed the recipes. Each one had to meet several criteria: that it fulfilled nutritional requirements, used authorized ingredients, optimized sensory quality, and was easily standardized and reproduced. The operative word on this list and the one that best describes army food is not *sensory* but *standardized*.

The standardized "Master Menu" dictated all army meals. This daily menu was issued from Fort Lee, Virginia, to be used by every army mess around the globe. To ensure that the U.S. Army everywhere was eating the exact same food, ice and ice cream factories were built abroad; sealand ships rushed food from the States to Europe; refrigerated trucks moved fresh vegetables to wherever they were needed. These global logistics allowed every mess to follow the menu called for by the home economists at Fort Lee.

It was this Master Menu that had dictated Elvis' first mess breakfast on that morning of March 25, 1958. Troops in Germany ate sausage and eggs, troops in Guam ate sausage and eggs, and Elvis Presley ate sausage and eggs.

During the next eight weeks of basic, Elvis was introduced to the Army version of all American cuisine, as well as to foods with a distinctively military cast.

Elvis the soldier politely pouring tea.

Recipes from the Master Menu of 1958

Many of the following recipes, all of which were served to Elvis, are heavy by today's standards, even by the standards of today's army (which emphasizes a lighter cuisine). Yet this anachronistic quality is what makes them so appealing—even, in their own way, classic.

General directions: "The successful Army cook is a soldier who prepares food well, serves it properly, and takes pride in his work" to quote from the army technical manual TM 10-405. Even without having undergone basic training or having kitchen police at your disposal, Elvis's army food can still be easily created. However, due to the portions, a mess size kitchen is helpful.

Military Cooking Tips

Military cooks have developed certain tricks of the trade:

☆ To make rice whiter and fluffier, add one teaspoon of lemon juice to each quart of water while cooking.

☆ To keep baked potatoes round and smooth, rub each potato with a little fat before baking and cut a small piece off one end; this permits the steam to escape during baking.

☆ Hard-boiled eggs placed in the center of a meat loaf will make a royal dish out of an ordinary loaf.

☆ For delicious and crisp celery, let stand in cold water to which one teaspoon sugar per quart of water has been added.

☆ To avoid wrinkled skins on baked apples, slit the skins in a few places before baking.

☆ To hold eggs together while poaching, add a few drops of vinegar to cooking water.

—U.S. Marines Corps, 1952
Yield for all recipes: Serves 100 troops

Omelet

150 eggs
8 quarts fresh milk
Salt and pepper to taste
2 pounds bacon drippings

Mix the eggs and milk, season, and whip well. Put the drippings or other fat into a baking pan, and when the fat begins to smoke pour in the egg mixture, not more than 3 inches deep. Bake in a medium oven.

To make a ham omelet, simply add 3 pounds of chopped ham to the egg mixture before cooking.

Recipe Source: **TM 10-405, The Army Cook**

Hotcakes

The Army Cook redundantly states that hotcakes should be "served hot," warning that if allowed to cool, they will become "tough and leathery."

12 pounds all-purpose flour
3 pounds sugar
4 ounces salt
12 ounces baking powder
36 eggs
6 quarts water
1 can evaporated milk
½ pound fat, melted

Sift together the flour, sugar, salt, and baking powder. Beat the eggs and add to water and evaporated milk. Turn the liquid mixture into the dry

(continued on next page)

mixture and add the melted fat. Then beat into a smooth batter. If the batter seems too thick, add a little more water or milk. Grease a hot griddle iron or clean stovetop with bacon rind or clean fat and pour out the batter, a spoonful at a time. Cook until nicely browned on both sides.

Recipe Source: TM 10-405

Fried Hominy Grits

The only difference between cornmeal and hominy grits is that cornmeal is of a finer grind. Elvis liked them both.

7 gallons water
4 ounces salt
10 pounds hominy grits

Bring salted water to a boil, add the hominy, and boil for about 20 minutes or until tender. Remove to the back part of the range and let simmer for about 40 minutes.

Remove the grits from the boiler, spread them about 1 inch deep in a well-greased pan, and allow them to cool. Cut the cooled grits in pieces about 2 inches square, roll them in flour, and fry the squares in deep fat. Serve hot with syrup or butter.

Recipe Source: TM 10-405

Navy Bean Soup of the U.S. Army

3 pounds dry navy beans
10 pounds soup bones
7 gallons water
2 cans tomatoes
1½ pounds bacon, diced and browned
Beef stock
Flour for thickening
Salt and pepper to taste

Thoroughly sort and wash the beans. Place them and the soup bones in water to cover and allow to simmer for about 5 hours or until the beans have gone to pieces and will pass through a colander. Ten minutes before serving add the tomatoes, the diced and browned bacon, and enough beef stock to make soup. Thicken with flour; add salt and pepper to taste. Serve with crackers.

Recipe Source: TM-1045

Soup cooked in the army style of the 1950s (though not today) is soup that utilizes all leftovers. As the army taught its cooks, "An inspector never finds a raw bone in the garbage of a well-conducted mess." The properly run mess would have used the bone in a soup.

Baked Ham with Raisin Sauce

45 pounds cured hams
Sugar (brown, white, or molasses)
1 teaspoon cloves per ham
1½ teacups flour
1 gallon beef stock
3 pounds well-washed raisins

Preheat the oven to 300°F. Cut off the hocks of the hams and reserve for later use as seasoning. Place the hams in a large kettle, cover with water, and boil slowly for 4½ hours or until the bone across the big end of the hams can be removed easily. Place the hams without this bone in a roasting pan. Remove the skin and make 3 cuts to a depth of ½ inch on the fat side of the hams. Fill the cuts with brown sugar (molasses or white sugar may be substituted). Stick a teaspoon of cloves in each ham. Place the hams in a slow oven (300–325°F.) and bake until golden brown. Remove the hams from the pan and put all of the juice in one large pot on top of the stove. Add the flour and stir well. Add 1 gallon of beef stock, stir again until it thickens, and add the raisins. Boil for ten minutes. Slice the ham and serve with the raisin sauce.

Recipe Source: **Army Mess Management Simplified**

Meat Loaf

35 pounds stew meat
6 eggs
10 pounds bread, ground
(fresh bread crumbs)
1 pound bacon, diced
1 pint water
1 pint ketchup
⅓ cup salt
3 tablespoons pepper
1 tablespoon thyme
2 garlic cloves, grated

Preheat the oven to 350°F. Grind the stew meat. Add the remaining ingredients and mix thoroughly. Make into 5-pound rolls. Place the loaves in a pan with just a little water. Brush the loaves with lard and cover them with greased brown paper. Bake for 90 minutes in a moderate oven.

Recipe Source: **TM 10-405**

Brown Betty

15 pounds bread or bread scraps
10 pounds sugar, caramelized
4 pounds currants or other
dried tart fruits
5 gallons water
Flour for thickening

Preheat oven to 350°F. Dice the bread into 1-inch cubes and brown in a slow oven. Add the caramelized sugar and the fruit to 5 gallons of water, thicken slightly with a flour batter, and pour over the diced bread. Bake in a medium oven about 20 minutes.

Recipe Source: **TM 10-405**

Apple Pie

Pie Crust

(makes 3 double 9-inch crusts)
1 pound all-purpose flour
⅛ ounce salt
8 ounces lard
¼ pint cold water

All ingredients should be thoroughly chilled before using. Mix the flour and salt with one-half the fat by chopping or cutting with a food chopper until the consistency of cornmeal. Then mix in the remainder of the fat by the same method, except that the fat should be cut in so as to leave the mixture in small pieces, about the size of a bean. Then add the cold water slowly while tossing the mixture with a fork. Then roll out the dough.

TM 10-405 notes that "for Army purposes, the best crust is the short flaky crust, a cross between homemade (which is very flaky) and commercial crust. A high proportion of shortening is used. Overhandling produces a tough crust."

Pie Filling

35 pounds apples
3 pounds sugar
Juice of 3 lemons
¾ ounce cinnamon

Peel, core, and cut the apples into eighths. Add the sugar, lemon juice, and cinnamon, and cook in a pan until the apples are medium soft, but not mushy. Avoid unnecessary stirring, which breaks the apples.

Make the pies with double crusts and bake about 40 minutes in a hot oven.

Recipe Source: **TM 10-405**

Lemonade

100 lemons
13 gallons ice water
7 pounds sugar
10 pounds ice

In a juicer, squeeze the juice from the lemons and add it to the water. Sweeten to taste with sugar and stir thoroughly before serving. Serve over ice.

Recipe Source: **TM 10-405**

Coffee

The army has very specific rules for making coffee, treating it with a seriousness the British reserve for afternoon tea. TM 10-405 flatly states, "Coffee is the most important beverage served in the Army." The army insists that its coffee be made with freshly roasted beans, which should be ground just before use. The cooks are ordered to discard used grounds. Says the army, "A good cup of coffee cannot be made when fresh coffee is added to grounds already used. Coffee should never be boiled."

Naturally, Elvis also ate the army's most ubiquitous foodstuff: Spam. Invented by the Hormel Company before World War II, it was quickly taken up by the army, which found its amorphous qualities appealing: Spam can be served hot or cold, fried or baked, in messes or on the go. Elvis and his fellow troops called Spam "ham that failed its physical."

Making his way down the mess line during basic, Elvis always piled his plate high with these foodstuffs and usually returned for seconds. Not that he liked everything he swallowed. Elvis wasn't a bean man, and he never would have ordered navy bean soup if it had been up to him. But the fact is, it wasn't. Elvis ate what was served, and he was so hungry that he slurped down the soup, along with anything else put in front of him. Basic training was tough, consisting of military exercises using rifles, tear gas, and bayonets. Time in between training was spent on marches, up to fifteen miles a day. As Elvis said, "Army chow's pretty good. But after a hard day, you could eat a rattlesnake."

Though the chow didn't bother Elvis, he was less happy with the chow lines. Even though he was now the King of Rock and Roll, he had to push along a tin tray like everyone else. It was as if he were back in the Humes High cafeteria. To make matters worse, the other GIs stared at him. Moreover, while Elvis stood waiting, GIs he barely knew would come and hit him up for a loan. Elvis was a pushover. He lent out twenty dollars at a time and more at payday. Since he didn't even know to whom he had lent the money, he wasn't paid back. Even so, he told his closest army buddy, Rex Mansfield, that he "was glad to help" the other guys.

The army did worse things than just making Elvis wait in line. The army pretended that Elvis was just an ordinary soldier. His only privilege was that he never had to pull KP and peel potatoes, and only because he had been in ROTC in high school. Elvis didn't mind his loss of privileges; he thought he was being a good citizen. But he still missed one thing from civilian life. It wasn't the food—he could always go to the Snow Queen off base with his girlfriend, Anita Wood. Elvis missed his mother.

Elvis managed to move his mother and

Elvis, "hungry enough to eat a rattlesnake."

Vernon off base from his new posting at Fort Hood, near Killeen, Texas. He chose a trailer for them, but this proved too small, so he then found a full-sized house. However, he spent all weekends apart from his family at a Quality Inn in Fort Worth. The attraction of the motel was more than its coffee shop. A large number of stewardesses stayed there. Nonetheless, food was always part of the fun: Elvis routinely made a pit stop at his army buddy Eddie Fadal's house in Waco on the way to the motel. Eddie's wife, La Nelle, was locally famous for her Bavarian chocolate cake. Elvis never limited himself to one slice; his serving size was the whole cake, which he could down in one sitting. Despite these snacks and the bulky army meals, the grueling marches kept Elvis in excellent physical condition. All in all, he lost twelve pounds during those first months in the army. He never looked better.

Alas, tragedy struck. As Elvis prepared to be shipped overseas, Gladys died. Some say it was of a broken heart over Elvis' departure. That her son had been drafted was hard enough on Gladys. That he was going to be sent abroad was just too much. She said shortly before dying, "I jes' can't see mahself over theah in a fereign country. It grieves me." His mother's death was the worst thing that had ever happened to Elvis.

Hordes of Memphis women arrived bearing food and drink for Gladys' wake— soggy sandwiches covered in Saran Wrap, shopping bags filled with cookies, and gelatin salads molded into wreaths. Soon the house was covered with greasy paper plates, old wrappers, and used paper cups. Before the situation got out of hand, Elvis' manager called off the wake, expelling the milling women.

Elvis completely ignored the crowd and the gifts of food. Upon seeing his mother's coffin, he opened the lid and in grief threw himself onto the body. When they were alone, he ran his own comb through Gladys' hair.

ELVIS ABROAD

Still in shock from his mother's death, Elvis, along with his unit, the Second Medium Tank Battalion, was shipped overseas to Bremen, Germany, on October 1, 1958. It was to be Elvis' only trip abroad. Elvis in Germany was like Elvis at home—trips to roller rinks, teenage girlfriends, lots of snacks. Elvis' journey had no impact, either short term or long term, on his cuisine, except to make him pine away for the foods of home.

After his ship docked in Germany, Elvis was immediately placed aboard a troop train with his eight-hundred-man battalion. The train headed south, arriving only after midnight at its destination—the barracks at Friedberg, in Hesse. The town was shrouded in damp fog; an ancient castle gloomily loomed through it. Elvis and the battalion slept in the base's receiving quarters. When they arose the next morning, the fog had not fully dispersed. The barracks consisted of seemingly endless gray buildings. The sinister atmosphere should have come as no surprise. During World War II, the barracks had been a base for the SS.

To Elvis' great relief, the food at this grim foreign base was still all-American. The standardized U.S. Army menu ensured that Elvis was served the same food as he was in Arkansas. The food on that first morning, only weeks after his mother's death, was particularly comforting to Elvis. It wasn't a breakfast his mother would have made, yet he found it soothing all the same. Nothing could be more American than corned beef hash, a national breakfast classic enjoyed by truckers in diners, matrons in Palm Beach, and Elvis in the German forests.

Corned Beef Hash

15 pounds potatoes
5 pounds onions
25 pounds cooked corned beef
1 garlic clove
Salt and pepper to taste
10 quarts beef stock

Preheat the oven to 450°F. Chop all the ingredients fine and add the beef stock until the mixture is the consistency of ordinary mush. Layer the mixture about 3 inches deep in a well-greased pan. Smooth the top and grease lightly. Bake in a quick oven for 90 minutes until done.

Recipe Source: **TM 10-405, The Army Cook**

During the next few weeks, Elvis immersed himself in his new army assignment as a tank scout. Scouts patrolled ahead of tanks to set up roadblocks. Elvis relished the prospect of being the first to encounter the enemy. He spent all his free time in a frantic search for lodging for his father and grandmother. Elvis would live off base with them—that Elvis was now in the army had never fully interfered with the Presleys' domestic routines.

Before Elvis had found a place to live, Vernon and Grandma arrived. He moved with them into a hotel in the nearby spa town of Bad Nauheim. They were soon forced to leave because he was too noisy for the elderly German guests taking the cure. Elvis finally found a house suitable for himself and his family, one that featured overstuffed furniture, six bedrooms, a living room with piano, an office, and—most important—a large kitchen.

At home, Elvis could enjoy all the pleasures of Grandma's kitchen. Here there were no chow lines, and Elvis was the mess sergeant. The food was not, like army chow, merely similar to the food from home but actually *was* the food he was raised on. Elvis' personal secretary, Elisabeth Mansfield, hired to answer the phone, knew how to cook, but she was rarely allowed to. She remembers that only "Grandma cooked because Elvis liked only certain foods and she would always fix his favorites." Vernon was sent to the PX to hunt down the necessary ingredients, all imported from America: Pepsi, Hormel chili, canned Vienna sausage, canned crowder peas, and peanut butter.

Elvis awoke at four-thirty each morning, waking up the rest of the household with him. Breakfast was served promptly. It never varied: two hard-fried eggs, round "cat's head biscuits," butter, jelly, bacon, ice-cold Georgia cling peaches, and scalding coffee. Elvis would spread the butter and jam on his opened biscuit, and

SALVAGED FATS

It takes three soldiers to carve the evening meal for a hungry regiment.

create "soaks" by dunking it all in his coffee. As an accompaniment, the bacon would be served with the peaches. Elvis liked to hold the sizzling bacon by the fat and nibble on the lean.

When Elvis was away at the base, "the boys" and members of his household would sneak out for foreign foods forbidden by Elvis if he were at home. Marinated wild boar, Wiener schnitzel,

and sauerbraten were quickly stuffed down by Elisabeth and Elvis' buddies Lamar and Red, before Elvis returned. No one mentioned a word about what they had just eaten.

When Elvis returned in the evening, he lay in bed reading *Mad* or *Cracked*. Grandma was down in the kitchen frying up a beloved snack from Memphis—a fried potato sandwich.

Fried Potato Sandwich

Elvis ate five of these at a sitting.

**½ pound bacon, browned
(save drippings)
2 russet potatoes,
sliced ¼ inch thick
Onions
White bread
Mustard**

Fry potatoes and onions in bacon grease till well done. Layer bacon, potatoes, and onions on white bread. Smear generously with mustard. Sear briefly under open grill.

Yield: **1 sandwich**

Elvis' first Christmas in Germany was Elvis' first without Gladys. Grandma felt too depressed to cook anything, so Elvis and his father dined at the post. The holiday only added to Elvis' gloom.

Elvis arrived at the mess, which was gaily decorated with red Christmas tinsel in an attempt to dress up the old SS interior. No one could fault the army for not really trying at Christmas. The 1958 Master Menu called for a lavish meal: shrimp cocktail with cocktail sauce, carrot sticks and olives, turkey with oyster stuffing, and pumpkin pie for dessert. Elvis hated shellfish and so wouldn't eat the oyster stuffing or the shrimp cocktail.

Because it was Christmas, the food was served on actual plates rather than tin trays, a right usually reserved for only what is called the "the permanent party" (enlisted staff) rather than draftees. Elvis was eating in a former SS base from plates made of the simplest china, and he still had to serve himself, but this dinner was Elvis' best in the army.

An Army Christmas Dinner

☆ SHRIMP WITH COCKTAIL SAUCE

☆ OLIVES AND CARROTS

☆ FRUIT CUP

☆ SWEET PICKLES

☆ TURKEY WITH OYSTER DRESSING

☆ CRANBERRY SAUCE

☆ SNOWFLAKE POTATOES

☆ CANDIED SWEET POTATOES

☆ BUTTERED ASPARAGUS TIPS

☆ WHOLE-KERNEL CORN

☆ PARKER HOUSE ROLLS AND BUTTER

☆ PUMPKIN PIE

☆ COFFEE

☆ SALTED NUTS

☆ HARD CANDY

☆ FRESH FRUIT

Turkey with Oyster Dressing

The army advises its chefs that the age of a turkey is indicated by the color of its feet: black up to a year, then pink between one and three. Young birds are recommended. Christmas turkey in the army is either served roasted or boiled.

50 pounds dressed and drawn turkey
4 gallons dry bread
6 onions
3 stalks celery
4 tablespoons salt
3 tablespoons pepper
8 eggs
1 tablespoon thyme
2 gallons oysters, shucked

Place the turkeys in a deep pot, cover with water, and boil until done or until the legs are tender. Remove from the fire and save the stock for soup.

To make the dressing, soak the bread until soft, then drain off the water. Chop the onions and the celery, and put them in a shallow pan with a little butter. Sauté the onions and celery for 15 minutes. Mix the celery and onions with the soaked bread, season with salt and pepper, then add the eggs and the thyme and the oysters. Put this dressing in a pan and bake in a hot oven for 30 minutes. Fill the turkey cavities with dressing, brush them with bacon grease or butter, and bake at 350° F. until nicely browned.

Recipe Source: **Army Mess Management Simplified** -

Shortly after Christmas, Elvis and his battalion were ordered into the field for maneuvers that took place at Grafenwöhr, deep in the German forests along the Czech border. Elvis conducted his anti-tank training exercises in an unheated jeep during a heavy blizzard.

During this winter exercise, Elvis got a kick out of warning the newer recruits about "the German snow snakes." He told them to watch out for these deadly snakes—they would slither out of their holes and into your sleeping bags as you slept. Elvis said that before you knew it, the snakes would crawl "into your tail-hole and freeze you to death." It was usually only at this point that the listener would realize the whole story was a joke.

Such jokes distracted Elvis from the painful conditions he and the battalion had to endure. There was no mess hall. Meals consisted of "food for combat situations," more commonly known as C rations.

These foodstuffs, designed literally for the battlefront, were the embodiment of cold war cuisine. The army itself, in a monograph published by its Subsistence Research Center, describes these compact meals in terms usually reserved for new weapons systems: "To stay abreast of new concepts and techniques of warfare, rations are under the constant scrutiny of the military analyst." The monograph continues, "New technologies have been brought to bear on foods for military use such as freeze-dehydration and radiation preservation."

Elvis was served his rations in a compact brown box. He would eagerly unfold it to reveal an assortment of canned food and accessory packets of cigarettes, matches, and a spoon. Best of all, there was also chewing gum.

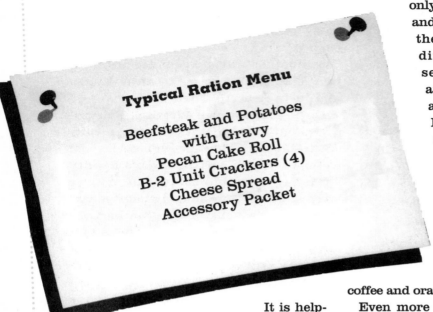

Typical Ration Menu

Beefsteak and Potatoes
with Gravy
Pecan Cake Roll
B-2 Unit Crackers (4)
Cheese Spread
Accessory Packet

It is helpful to remember that these canned "meals" could have been in storage for years. Advanced food preservation technologies meant that some of Elvis' rations dated from the Second World War.

France presented a different set of gastronomic challenges for the King. He took a little-known trip to Paris while in the army, staying at the Hôtel Prince de Galles. He strolled out the front door telling his entourage, "Before we make all these plans for Paris let's just try her out." He then set out for a café on the Champs-Elysées. Before you could say "jack rabbit," Elvis was mobbed. He was unable to order, and forced to make a slow retreat to the hotel.

Elvis spent the next ten days in a routine that was night and day from the army. He arose at 8:00 P.M. and headed for the Lido, where he once did a slow dance with Esther Williams. Later he would hit the 4 O'Clock Club, taking several of its "Blue Belle girls" to his hotel suite each dawn. Food played only a secondary role on the trip and was designed not to get in the way. Elvis restricted his dining to one meal a day, served each evening upon awakening. Since Elvis had absolutely no interest in French food, his Paris hotel served him breakfast à l'américain rather than continental. Except for the time of day it was served and the fact that it arrived via room service, this Paris breakfast could easily have been a mess breakfast: eggs and ham, bacon, coffee and orange juice.

Even more exciting than Paris and its breakfasts was what awaited Elvis on his return to Germany. It was not a foodstuff but an army brat. In his living room in Bad Nauheim, Elvis met the woman of his dreams; she was the most beautiful fourteen-year-old he had ever set eyes upon. Priscilla Beaulieu would have more effect upon Elvis than anyone save his mother.

After a year and a half in Germany, and nearly two years in the army, Elvis was finally sent home to be discharged. He planned a vacation at the Fontainebleau Hotel in Miami to recuperate from his experience in the service. Before he was discharged, he spent half a week at Fort Dix in New Jersey, mustering out of the army. Army cuisine, which Elvis had found so reassuring, even nurturing, still had a few surprises up its sleeve. During that last week, he enjoyed one of the army's most soothing recipes. Creamed chipped beef on toast is also the most notorious. It's better known in the army by its other name:

Shit on a Shingle

2 pounds fat, butter preferred
1 pound flour
4 cans evaporated milk
4 gallons beef stock
7 pounds chipped or dried beef
2 bunches parsley, chopped fine
½ ounce pepper
12 pounds (130 slices) bread, toasted

Melt the fat in a large pot and add the flour. Cook for a few minutes to brown the flour. Add the milk and the beef stock, stirring constantly to prevent lumping. Add the dried beef and cook 5 minutes. Add the parsley and the pepper, and serve hot on toast.

Some people claim the army ruined Elvis. In 1977, when told that Elvis had died, John Lennon retorted, "Elvis died the day he went into the army." Elvis, though no doubt injured by the army experience, was not compromised by his military service. All around him in Germany, the Germans were engaging in what is known as *Fressenkrankheit*, or the eating disease. Recovering from postwar starvation, Germans were literally stuffing themselves to death on sausages, chocolate bars, potatoes, or other newly abundant food supplies. Much as this behavior resembled Elvis' in later life, Elvis was in no way tempted by it. During his entire stay overseas in Germany, he remained faithful to American cuisine, refusing even to sample what he truly hated most—German food.

Elvis dining in Germany. Notice the Coca-Cola.

DINNER AT ELVIS' COOK'S HOUSE

Pauline Nicholson fixed me dinner at her house when I was in Memphis tracing Elvis' meals. Since she was a night cook at Graceland (there were several day cooks), and since Elvis was a nocturnal person, it's safe to assume she was the busiest person in the mansion. Pauline started working for Elvis in 1964 (she remembers the exact day—August 4). She was to remain with Elvis for the rest of his life.

Pauline, me, and Hunt's Ketchup.

Today, Pauline still lives near Graceland in a cozy, well-kept home. Pauline looks about fifty, but she indicated she is actually substantially older, though no one would ever guess. When I arrived, Pauline was just starting up dinner, so she sat me down in the kitchen with a big glass of soda until the meal was ready. She opened and poured several cans of Coke into my enormous glass until it was full. She told me this was how Elvis liked his drinks served, in a giant-sized glass filled all the way, with lots of little pieces of ice, too, to chew on. This was the first thing Pauline told me about Mr. P., as Pauline referred to Elvis.

Pauline was making me some of Elvis' favorites for dinner—green beans, mashed potatoes, crowder peas, and best of all, "ugly steak." Ugly steak was what Elvis called chicken fried steak, because when you fry it, it bubbles and curls up and generally looks really ugly. I had been expecting only a peanut butter and banana sandwich but Pauline insisted she could hardly just cook me a sandwich for dinner.

When the pots on the stove were all bubbling, Pauline took a break from cooking to sit down and talk. She cleared off the bananas and newspapers covering part of the table to make room for herself. There was a lot of stuff in the kitchen because Pauline has a large family, and she does all the cooking. Several of her friendly and engaging children looked on while we spoke, including a daughter who is a professional gospel singer.

"When I first met him, it was on a Saturday night. I didn't know if I would be able to work for a star." Pauline was originally from Oxford, Mississippi, and had previously cooked at several night-clubs. "Joe Esposito [a friend of Elvis'] had explained to me that Elvis liked the hot bread and he liked his watermelon and stuff cut into bite-size pieces. That's the way I did his watermelon that night. Then Elvis came in. And he loved the watermelon. And that's also the way I did his meat from then on. I thought, I prob-ably can't cook to suit him. But it never was a problem all the years I was there."

Pauline got up again to tend to the dinner. As I watched, Pauline took a large piece of top sirloin and scored it repeatedly with a knife before frying to make sure it was tender. She told me she always used to be nervous that the meat wouldn't be tender enough for Elvis, so at Graceland she used a mallet to pound the steak into tenderness. She made fresh green beans, snapping the ends off, while she opened the crowder peas from a can—Allen's—which is how she usually made them for Elvis. From across the kitchen, Pauline asked me if I liked onions. I told her yes, but asked why. She told me she boiled the peas with a lit-tle onion, but because she didn't know if I liked onions or not, she had already strained them out. That shows you just how thoughtful Pauline is.

When Elvis was at Graceland, he requested that Pauline work seven days a week. She was so busy that, in order to feed her husband, she would have to try to make him dinner while at work. "I might have made me some peas or cooked a roast. Elvis would come in and start eating my dinner, he didn't know the difference, and I wouldn't have any dinner left at all. I'd just bring on home whatever I could find."

Pauline told me what Elvis was like by explaining how he ordered his breakfast, the first meal she would make when she arrived in the late afternoon. "When I went to work at five o'clock in the evening, he might call down for food [on the internal phone] but he would always take time out first to speak to me. He'd always say, will ya? 'Hi Pauline, will ya fix me some breakfast.' I'd say, 'Sure, Mr. P., what do you want?' Sometimes he might say sausage, sometimes he might say bacon, and I knew to fix the scram-bled eggs well done. And some biscuits."

At long last, dinner was ready. Pauline brought over the sizzling-hot skillet bear-ing the "ugly steak," which had contorted itself into a knot like a muscle in pain. But its light crust was a russet brown and I knew the steak was going to be not only authentic but delicious.

Pauline served the vegetables in their pale green and red pots. The pots were from Graceland! Priscilla gave them to Pauline when she redecorated the kitchen in 1965. And then Pauline told me that my plate, which was white with faint gold tracing, was from Graceland, too. I picked it up and looked at the mark underneath. Sure enough, it was gen-uine Noritake porcelain, the Bucking-ham pattern, Elvis' favorite.

As she promised, Pauline cut the steak into little pieces for me. This was always done at Graceland in the kitchen. Pauline insisted on following the exact tradition-al procedures.

Pauline asked me if I wanted ketchup

for my chicken fried steak, because I was from "up North" (in the South, it is served without ketchup). I truthfully told her no, but asked what brand they used at Graceland. I was curious in part because I once worked at a ketchup factory—Hunt's—in Bridgeton, New Jersey.

"I don't know about the brand," Pauline said. "A lot of times they got Heinz and sometimes Del Monte, no telling. They didn't stick with one thing. Sometimes they used the brand I have here in my kitchen." Pauline couldn't remember its name. She silently padded over to the fridge, where she found a big plastic bottle of Hunt's.

I tasted Pauline's crowder peas, which were moist yet firm, not gloppy the way you usually find them in restaurants. The onion-butter broth Pauline fixed them in

accounted for their comparative delicacy. She told me that the broth "takes the canned taste out." Nestled on my plate between the steak and the peas were the green beans, which were thinly sliced lengthwise. Most people prefer their beans crunchy, but not Elvis. He liked them soft and these were cooked real soft, Elvis style. Pauline told me her secret: she had cooked the beans for two hours.

I couldn't overlook the mountain of mashed potatoes on my plate. Pauline had mashed them from scratch. I was afraid they were going to be what is politely called "stick-to-your-ribs food"—in another words, glutinous. But these mashed potatoes weren't gummy at all. The huge amount of butter Pauline used transformed the spuds into something ethereal.

Elvis' favorite bread.

The dinner was a bit salty, but I couldn't help getting carried away by it. I had set out a year before on a quest to eat what Elvis ate. In Pauline's kitchen on a sultry Memphis night, I came closer to my ambition than I had ever dreamed possible.

"I wasn't swift enough to get going on a dessert before you arrived," Pauline apologized to me from across the kitchen. This was fine with me because I'd already eaten more than enough. I asked Pauline what the King's favorite dinner was. "I don't hardly know. But anyway, what you had was one of them."

We retired to her living room. I sat on one of the ornate sofas, their pillows covered in protective plastic. A large ornamental swan graced the coffee table. The tone of the evening grew more solemn. Pauline told me about the last time she ever spoke to Elvis. Elvis had been promising Pauline a car for a while. "At six-fifteen A.M. Monday he called down. He said, 'Pauline, will you call your husband for me. I said sure. I said, 'Oh! Mr. P., he's already left. He gets off work at six.' He called again at six-fifteen Tuesday morning for my husband. But he had already left. I feel he was gonna tell him to go and select a car for me. Elvis didn't call again. And then he was gone." Pauline was silent. She wasn't thinking about the car Elvis promised her. She was thinking about how much Elvis had cared about her and that now he was dead. It had been more than fifteen years, but her eyes still welled up with tears.

Then Pauline remembered another story, strange but cheering. "There would come a time when I was in the kitchen, I might just take a walk. Just sitting around the kitchen I get sleepy or tired sometimes. I might get up and walk down to the music room [with the gold piano] and then later when I would come back to the kitchen, I would get a phone call. When I answered the phone it would be him. 'Pauline.' I said, 'Yes, Mr. P.' 'I seen you a while ago in the music room.' 'Oh, did you really?' 'Yes.'"

Elvis had seen Pauline on Graceland's closed-circuit video system, which scanned every room. The monitor was at the foot of Elvis' bed. Then Elvis said to her on the phone, "And Pauline, you look just like my mother. You even walk like my mother."

Pauline is a black woman with white hair and Gladys Presley was a white woman with black hair. It's not altogether surprising that Elvis would compare his cook to his mother. I looked at Pauline again. She was about to laugh. And then when she smiled, it was clearly true. She had Gladys' jolly smile, and bright eyes, and desire to nurture.

Pauline continued, "One time he called me, up to his bedroom, he wanted me to stand up there on the bed. And he told me, 'Now look up there.' His mother's picture sat on top there. He said, 'Look up there at Mama's picture. Now look at her. Don't you look just like Mama.'"

GROCERY SHOPPING FOR ELVIS

In order to make Elvis' Graceland favorites, you'll need to shop as if you were shopping for Elvis. Shopping for the King was like shopping for no one else.

Most people, when they go grocery shopping, glide down the aisles of the supermarket wearing glazed expressions as they concentrate on their shopping list.

The Muzak only adds to the Stepford Wife–like quality of the supermarket experience. The shoppers are trying to keep their composure in the face of the distracting and enticing scene around them—the smell of the candy display, the luminescent glow of the frozen food department with its many varieties of ice cream, the strange dog treats in the pet section. The shoppers must press on amidst these distractions, propelled by their obligation to follow their shopping lists.

A grocery list for shoppers who are concerned about their own health and the health of their loved ones has selections from each of the four food groups. The health-conscious shopper's cart is loaded with their favorite brands—of low-fat cottage cheese, iron-packed spinach, fibrous flaked cereal, skimmed milk, and prunes. But there are also consumers who are not so health conscious. These, too, follow a list with their own favorite brands. Their carts are loaded with fried pork skins, family packs of corn chips, Crackerjack, Cheese Whiz, and other delicacies.

Both groups of shoppers meet in the checkout line. The lists have been marked off. They thumb through the *National Enquirer* and *Redbook* for sex, cooking, and diet tips while they are waiting. They present coupons and hope the bill isn't more than expected. What both groups have in common is financial concerns. Neither could buy all they wanted, of either oat muffins or Corn Nuts. There are always limitations. Nutrition may or may not come first to all shoppers, but budget almost always does.

Grocery shopping for Elvis, on the other hand, had no limitations. It resembled the prize on the game show where you have fifteen minutes to stuff your cart with anything you want. "Elvis shopping" was frenzied. The four major food groups were ignored. Coupons didn't count. Specials were irrelevant; even brand names weren't important. Speed was everything and so was bulk. The larders at Graceland had to be continually replenished.

Elvis, of course, didn't do the shopping himself. The pilgrimage to the Piggly Wiggly was undertaken by Aunt Delta until she took sick, and then later by the cooks. The weekly cost, even in the 1960s, was about five hundred dollars. What is striking about Elvis' grocery list is that the favored brand names kept changing. A Graceland staff member who did the shopping remembers, "There's no telling what brand they got. They didn't stick with one thing. I guess, whatever they got to first, that's what they bought." She adds, "They didn't have to get nothing on sale. Whatever they wanted is whatever they got." All that was important was that the food pipeline was kept open, that the goods kept coming.

Though the brand names always varied, the foods never did. Elvis, an accidental tourist (all his hotel rooms had to have their windows covered with tin foil, just like his bedroom at Graceland), demanded the same foods on the road as at home. Marty Lacker, capo of the Memphis Mafia (the nickname for Elvis' entourage), wrote out the shopping list Elvis required in each city on the road. The shopping list has been put on display at the Elvis Hall of Fame in Gatlinburg, Tennessee. There you can buy a mimeographed copy, which contains some of the following items that had to be kept in the "kitchen and house for Elvis—AT ALL TIMES—EVERY DAY."

ELVIS' SHOPPING LIST

- ✓ FRESH, LEAN, UNFROZEN GROUND ROUND MEAT
- ✓ ONE CASE REGULAR PEPSI
- ✓ ONE CASE ORANGE DRINKS
- ✓ ROLLS (HOT ROLLS—BROWN 'N' SERVE)
- ✓ CANS OF BISCUITS (AT LEAST SIX)
- ✓ HAMBURGER BUNS
- ✓ PICKLES
- ✓ POTATOES AND ONIONS
- ✓ ASSORTED FRESH FRUITS
- ✓ CANS OF SAUERKRAUT
- ✓ WIENERS
- ✓ AT LEAST THREE BOTTLES OF MILK AND 1/2 &1/2 CREAM
- ✓ THIN, LEAN BACON
- ✓ MUSTARD
- ✓ PEANUT BUTTER
- ✓ FRESH, HAND-SQUEEZED COLD ORANGE JUICE
- ✓ BANANA PUDDING (TO BE MADE EACH NIGHT)
- ✓ INGREDINTS FOR MEAT LOAF AND SAUCE
- ✓ BROWNIES (TO BE MADE EACH NIGHT)
- ✓ ICE CREAM—VANILLA AND CHOCOLATE
- ✓ SHREDDED COCONUT
- ✓ FUDGE COOKIES
- ✓ GUM (SPEARMINT, DOUBLEMINT, JUICY FRUIT— 3 EACH)
- ✓ CIGARS (EL PRODUCTO DIAMOND TIPS & EL PRODUCTO ALTAS)
- ✓ CIGARETTES
- ✓ DRISTAN
- ✓ SUPER ANAHIST
- ✓ CONTAC
- ✓ SUCRETS (ANTIBIOTIC RED BOX)
- ✓ FEENAMINT GUM
- ✓ MATCHES (FOUR TO FIVE BOOKS)

- ✓ MAZOLA OIL
- ✓ SHASTA DIET DRINKS: PEACH, RASPBERRY, AND BLACK CHERRY

Whenever Elvis went out, he traveled with a cigar box (carried by a member of his entourage) which always contained:

- ✓ WOOD-TIPPED CIGARS
- ✓ PLAIN CIGARS
- ✓ TUBE OF BLISTEX
- ✓ TAREYTON CIGARETTES (TWO PACKS)
- ✓ SMALL BOTTLE OF DRISTAN
- ✓ SMALL BOTTLE OF SUPER ANAHIST
- ✓ ONE CARD PACKAGE OF CONTAC
- ✓ ONE TIN OF ANTIBIOTIC SUCRETS
- ✓ TWO SMALL BOTTLES OF EYEDROPS
- ✓ TWO EMERY BOARDS AND FINGERNAIL FILE
- ✓ MATCHES
- ✓ ONE JAR OF OCCULINE EYE PADS (IN LOS ANGELES ONLY)
- ✓ GUM
- ✓ SOUR BALLS
- ✓ GLOVES AND SUNGLASSES

The list is generally imprecise about brand names because the shoppers switched brands so often. However, the kitchen tended to favor the following:

- ✓ CRISCO
- ✓ SEALTEST BUTTERMILK

The cooks who went grocery shopping for Elvis never bought him his favorite beverage, regular Pepsi. It wasn't that Elvis didn't drink Pepsi, but rather that he drank much too much of it to buy it at the supermarket. Instead, Elvis had cases delivered directly by the "drink truck"; Graceland was a regular stop on the delivery route of the Pepsi distributor.

THE MEALS

In his first film, *Love Me Tender* (1956), Elvis played a farmboy who was raised on a picturesque Southern homestead. During filming, Elvis decided that in his life offscreen he needed a big house in the country just like the one in the movie (he was then living in a suburban ranch house on Memphis' Audubon Drive). Before he left for the army, Elvis scoured the countryside outside Memphis until he found the house of his dreams. It had eighteen rooms and a four-car garage on fourteen rolling acres. The house also had a name: Graceland.

After he was discharged from the Army, Elvis returned to his rock and roll palace. Here Elvis cuisine was to come into its own. At Graceland, the palate (and sensibility) that had been developing for years in rural Tupelo, and then as a teen in Memphis, was to reach its full-blown, mature form.

At Graceland, Elvis had cooks on duty twenty-four hours a day. He could lie in bed and phone down for whatever he wanted while they stood in the kitchen, chopping knife in hand, ready for action. The kitchen these cooks worked in was no different from one found in an ordinary suburban house, down to the checked curtains and normal-sized appliances. The cooks—Pauline, Mary, Alberta, Lottie, and Nancy—were devoted to the King. They handled his substantial orders, which came in bursts throughout the night, with the professionalism of air-traffic controllers handling rush hour at an international airport.

At Graceland, Elvis designed a dining room that outdid Las Vegas at its glitziest. Elvis' touch was visible everywhere. He covered the walls with smoked mirrors and installed an elaborate chandelier. The focal point of the room was the dining table, and the one Elvis chose was extraordinary: ten feet long and topped in smoked mirror. What made the room most "Elvis" was the thirty-six-inch color TV, which could be seen from the table (with unobstructed views). It was always kept on.

Elvis rarely ate in Graceland's dining room; sit-down dinners were too formal and convention-bound for him. Instead, as he did with everything, Elvis ate where he pleased, usually in the jungle room. Filled with Kon Tiki chairs, rabbit-fur throw pillows, and softly lit by the glow emitted from the fake-fur lampshades, the jungle room was Elvis' real dining room. He favored a chair in front of the room's bubbling waterfall, where he could savor his dinner in peace.

Elvis also ate breakfast in bed, and lunch and dinner, too. Indeed, his bed was Elvis' personal café. He designed the bedroom to suit his needs—the windows were permanently sealed and shuttered and the air conditioner was never turned off. Propped up in bed in this dark chamber, Elvis could eat morning, noon, and night, oblivious to the outside world.

Graceland and its rooms are just a

backdrop, though a magnificent one, setting the stage for the main players: the biscuits, potatoes, and chicken fried steak. Simple yet succulent, the food Elvis ate at Graceland was in the tradition of the food of his youth. Despite his great wealth, Elvis favored meals that were both innocent and fabulous, a choice that reveals much more than his taste in food. It describes his character.

How to Cook Elvis Style

Elvis cuisine has its own secrets, its own style, its own special way of doing things. Here are the basic tips necessary to reproduce that seemingly elusive Graceland dining style.

NAPKINS. Elvis always used a towel.

GLASSWARE. Elvis drank from gold-plated glasses. If Elvis used clear ones, they had to be huge, large enough to hold several cans of soda.

CHINA. The place settings at Graceland were Noritake china, Buckingham pattern, manufactured in Japan. Elvis and Priscilla purchased them at Memphis' Goldsmith's department store.

CUTLERY. Elvis enjoyed eating picnic style. However, he fastidiously used a knife and fork to eat his peanut butter and banana sandwiches.

COOKING TIME. When you think the food is done, cook it some more. Elvis liked his food burnt. Coincidentally (or maybe not), Elvis's favorite word of endorsement was "burnt." "That's burnt, man," he would say, which could indicate either a good steak or a good performance.

HOW TO SERVE. At Graceland, service was always a serious affair. The food was never served French style, with a maid passing dishes from guest to guest. Au contraire, at dinner parties at least, the food was served family style, with the guests passing the dishes themselves. Usually, however, the food was served Elvis style: heaping plates prepared in the kitchen were brought to Elvis in his thronelike Kon Tiki chair in front of the jungle room's waterfall.

SEASONING. Use salt and plenty of it. Elvis loved salt. He always salted his food before he tasted it. The cook once tried to stop him as he picked up his salt-shaker. Grabbing his hand, she warned him, "Mr. P., wait, the pork chop's seasoned pretty high already." He tasted it just to make sure, then went ahead and salted it some more anyway.

BEFORE SERVING. Cut up all the food into bite-size pieces; this is the cardinal rule of Elvis cuisine. And once you've served it to your guest of honor, never, ever, poke at the guest's plate. Only Elvis was allowed to touch the food on his plate. He never shared.

The cooks, in order to cut Elvis' steaks into little tiny bites, had to touch the King's food. They were concerned Elvis might mistakenly think they were playing with it (Elvis could see everything going on in the kitchen on closed-circuit

TV). Yet Elvis never said a word about it. As a member of the kitchen staff put it, "I wasn't playing with his food, I was cutting it up. He was up there looking down here, and if he didn't want it done, he would have done told me. Because of the closed circuit, he could see what you're doing, inside and outside. It wasn't anything strange to him."

AMBIENCE. Make sure the TV is always on.

Breakfast

When Pauline Nicholson arrived for work at the mansion at 5:00 P.M., Elvis would telephone her in the kitchen for his breakfast. Sometimes he wanted sausage and eggs, other times he wanted bacon and eggs; but he always wanted biscuits buttered heavy.

Pauline would fix his plate with the sausage or bacon and eggs. The biscuits went on a separate little bread plate. Planning ahead, she had already squeezed his orange juice. Elvis liked it served in a glass milk bottle, not in a pitcher, which was reserved for scalding black coffee.

Elvis ate breakfast in what was called the office, or in Lisa Marie's room, or—most often—in bed. Pauline put everything on a platter and carried it upstairs. Elvis had a tray that fit across his lap, where Pauline would set down the breakfast.

Sometimes Elvis might drop off to sleep before finishing. Pauline would find him under his tray. So as not to wake him, she would tiptoe in and remove the dishes.

When he got up, he might call down again and start over with a new breakfast.

Elvis ate "breakfast" around the clock. We define an Elvis breakfast by the foods consumed, not by the time of day. Pauline remembers that when she left in the morning at 8:00 A.M., Elvis would order the same thing as a snack before retiring that she ate for breakfast the night before—sausage, eggs, and biscuits.

Note: All recipes have been developed from the cook's original verbal directions.

Eggs Elvis Style

Pauline says, "It doesn't take long to cook them. You can cook the eggs in less than five minutes. When the skillet is hot, you can cut the heat off. With that being an electric stove at Graceland, it would be plenty hot enough to cook eggs.

"Sometimes he'd want an egg omelet with cheese," Pauline remembers. "We'd have some bell peppers cut up, always kept some bell pepper cut up 'cause you never know when he'd call for that."

**6 large eggs
Salt (a lot)
Pepper (to taste)
2 tablespoons butter**

In a medium mixing bowl beat together the eggs, the salt, and the pepper. Heat the butter in a large skillet over medium heat and add the beaten eggs. Let cook without stirring until the eggs are completely set. With a spatula, flip to cook the other side. Cook until well browned.

Yield: **1 serving**

Omelet Variation

1 green pepper, seeded and chopped
½ cup chopped American cheese
6 large eggs
2 tablespoons butter
Salt (a lot)
Pepper (to taste)

Add the green pepper and the cheese to the eggs, salt, and pepper. Follow above directions for making Eggs Elvis Style.

Sausage and Bacon

Elvis always ate his eggs with sausage or bacon, at least a half pound of sausage, sometimes a lot more. They were prepared in a separate skillet from the omelet. The cook remembers, "A pound of sausage or a pound of bacon was just a meal for him."

Sausage
½ pound Country Pride sausages
Fry in skillet till brown, draining grease.

Bacon
1 pound King Cotton bacon
Fry in skillet till burnt, draining grease.

Cereal

Every once in a while, Elvis wanted cereal with his bacon. His cereal of choice was shredded wheat.

3 to 4 bowls whole milk
3 to 4 bowls shredded wheat

Pour the milk over the shredded wheat. Add plenty of sugar.

Oatmeal

Elvis wouldn't eat instant oatmeal. It always had to be made from scratch.

4 cups water
2 cups Old-Fashioned Quaker Oats
½ stick (4 tablespoons) butter
Milk
Sugar

Bring the water to a rolling boil over high heat in a medium saucepan. Stir in the oats and cook, stirring, about 5 minutes or until very thick. Stir in 2 tablespoons of the butter and place in serving dishes. Top with milk and sugar. Per Pauline, make sure it's not soupy—the thicker the better. As a last touch, Pauline always dotted butter around the edge of Elvis' oatmeal dish, using close to an additional ½ stick.

Buttermilk Biscuits

The buttermilk biscuits Pauline made at Graceland are the most basic and the best. Archetypes of what a biscuit should be, these are made from only three ingredients: flour, buttermilk, and shortening. Elvis liked his biscuits hot, split open, and smothered with butter.

2 cups Gold Medal self-rising flour
1 tablespoon baking powder
½ teaspoon salt
½ cup Crisco
⅔ cup buttermilk

Preheat the oven to 425°F. Grease a large baking sheet with additional Crisco.

Place the flour and other dry ingredients in a large mixing bowl. With two knives or a pastry cutter, work in the Crisco until the mixture forms fine crumbs. Stir in the buttermilk with a fork until just mixed. The batter will be somewhat sticky. Turn the dough onto a lightly floured surface. Knead briefly. Using a rolling pin, roll out the dough about ½ inch thick. Cut the dough with a biscuit cutter (which is what they did at Graceland; if you don't have one, use a cookie cutter). Place the biscuits on a greased baking sheet and bake for about 15 minutes or until browned nicely.

Yield: **12 biscuits**

"You couldn't take all the biscuits in there to the table at one time 'cause then they'd get cold," Pauline recalls. She always had a second batch of ten waiting, made just after the first, so that hot biscuits were always available for Elvis' table. "I could go to the door and peep through the little peephole there, in the door between the kitchen and the dining room. When the bread got a little low, I'd go ahead and take some more in and pick up the cold bread. He didn't like cold bread. He only ate the hot bread."

Elvis ate between six and eight hot biscuits with each meal. They were served without gravy.

Dinner

Let's begin by clearing up any confusion about what was Elvis' favorite dinner: he didn't have one single favorite. Instead he went through various food crazes, craving the same dinner for months on end—burritos, hamburgers, or yogurt—only to suddenly cast the old favorite aside for something new that tickled his palate. In general, he favored familiarity over novelty, choosing Southern foods. As Elvis' cook says, "He just loved his green beans, and crowder peas, and creamed potatoes. He kind'a stuck with those things."

The kitchen usually started "bringing up" his dinner at about ten. Elvis, who had finished breakfast at five or six, was hungry again. In the Southern way, Elvis also called lunch "dinner," but in any case, "lunch" didn't fit into his nocturnal schedule. Following dinner he might play racquetball or see a movie before going back to sleep again in the early morning as the sun came up. Before retiring, there was time for a second breakfast or a second dinner or a snack.

Preparing dinner for Elvis was a twenty-four-hour operation at Graceland. Pies and pie crusts were baked through the night, meats cooked, plates washed, tables set. Then that special call would come in to the kitchen—it was dinnertime!

Here is what Elvis ate for dinner:

Chicken Fried Steak
a.k.a. Ugly Steak

When Pauline was pressed to name the dish Elvis asked for most frequently, she responded without hesitation, "Top sirloin." By this, she meant chicken fried sirloin steak.

1 pound top sirloin steak, pounded with a meat tenderizer
1 garlic clove cut in half
½ teaspoon salt
½ teaspoon pepper
½ teaspoon onion powder
⅓ cup all-purpose flour
Mazola oil for frying

Rub the steak with the garlic halves; discard the garlic. Sprinkle the meat with the salt, pepper, and onion powder. Place the flour on a plate and dredge both sides of the steak in it. Shake the excess flour from the steak.

Heat the oil in an iron skillet, using enough to cover the steak. When the oil is about 350°F. throw in the steak. Fry until brown and turn to brown other side, until well done. Remove to warm platter. Before serving, cut into tiny bite-size pieces.

At Graceland, they used a diamond-shaped meat tenderizer to beat the meat. Pauline always tried not to bread the steak too heavily. "I just floured it lightly," says Pauline. "I didn't try to put on a whole bunch of flour. Then I slapped some of the flour off it."

Make sure you fry until well done. "He liked all meats well done," Pauline remembers.

Gravy

"We didn't have to worry about gravy," Pauline reminisces. "He wasn't a gravy fan unless it was out of town. When we had steak and creamed potatoes, he might like a little bit of gravy on that.

"When you fry your chicken, your steak, whatever, when you get through frying, you've got enough of brown, the substance that's left in the bottom of the skillet. Cook it down and let it get thick, keep stirring until it gets as thick as you want."

After frying your chicken or steak, pour off all but 2 to 3 tablespoons of the fat. Add 2 to 3 cups of water and stir up all the browned bits on the bottom of the skillet. Let the mixture boil over medium-high heat, stirring constantly, until mixture becomes very thick. Season with salt and pepper.

Pauline drizzled the substance over the creamed potatoes. "If I wanted to fix a lot and didn't have very much of that brown in the skillet, I added flour and let it brown," she says.

Sometimes Pauline put onions in her gravy. "He liked his onions and he liked onion gravy on his hamburgers."

Onion Gravy

Follow directions for regular gravy, left, first adding 1 medium onion, chopped, to the remaining fat. Cook, stirring, until the onion is soft, about 4 minutes. Then add water and follow directions for regular gravy.

Mashed Potatoes for Elvis

Elvis often ate his steak accompanied by buttery mashed potatoes. Gravy for the potatoes is optional.

5 pounds white potatoes
1 teaspoon salt
4 tablespoons butter, cut into small pieces
½ teaspoon pepper

Wash the potatoes well and peel them. Place the potatoes in a large pot and cover with cold water. Add the salt. Bring to a boil and then reduce to a simmer. Simmer about 30 minutes or until the potatoes are very tender. Drain well and return the potatoes to the pot. Mash the potatoes with a hand masher, adding the butter and the pepper. If desired, add additional salt to taste.

Yield: **Enough for Elvis**

Crowder Peas

Pauline always cooked the peas in a butter broth to add flavor. "In Elvis' lifetime they used to use a lot of streak of lean [a type of fat]. You could put it in the water instead of the butter. But in the later years, I got to a place where we would just use the butter. He always liked butter."

2 tablespoons butter
1 medium onion cut into pieces
½ cup water
1 can Allen's crowder peas, drained

Combine the butter, onion, and ½ cup water in a medium saucepan over medium-high heat. Bring to a boil, cover, and cook 10 minutes. Uncover, strain out the onion, and add the peas. Cook 5 minutes or even longer.

Pauline adds, "After they start boiling, you can slow it down, let them simmer about thirty minutes. By that time you can have your bread done if you're gonna cook some. Then you just serve."

Fresh Green Beans

6 tablespoons unsalted butter
2 medium onions, quartered
2 to 3 cups boiling water
1 pound fresh green beans, washed, ends snapped

Melt the butter in a large heavy skillet over medium-high heat. Add the onions and 2 cups of water and cook about 4 minutes or until the onion is soft. Strain. Add beans and remaining boiling water to cover beans if necessary and cook, simmering, for 10 minutes (or up to 2 hours for Elvis style) or until the beans are done to your liking.

Yield: 4 servings

You don't necessarily have to strain out the onions. Sometimes they were left in for Elvis, who, according to Pauline, "loved onions all right."

I asked Pauline how long she cooked the beans.

"It takes about two hours," she told me.

"Two hours?"

"I don't time anything, I just fix up something and go ahead."

Greens

Graceland had a garden in the back. The yard people grew and tended greens there. The cooks could pick fresh greens when they needed to, thoroughly washing them before cooking.

1 bunch poke salad
Water to cover greens
1 bunch mustard greens
1 bunch turnip greens
1 bunch collards
2 tablespoons bacon grease
1 medium chunk salt pork

(continued on next page)

Wash and "clean up the greens." Separate out the poke salad and mix together the other greens. Boil the poke salad by itself for 10 minutes first. Pour off the water and rinse the poke salad in a colander. Boil more water, adding a little bit of bacon grease and salt pork. Add the poke salad as well as the mixture of other greens. Strain out the salt pork before serving. (Elvis did not eat salt pork.)

Elvis ate the greens with corn bread and sliced tomatoes, just as he had done as a child. The difference was, he now had meat, too.

Corn Bread

At Graceland, Pauline fixed corn bread two different ways. If Elvis was in a hurry, the fastest way was to fry it on top of the oven in a skillet, creating a sort of pancake. Elvis referred to them as "corn cakes." Corn cakes were eaten between meals.

If Elvis was having a proper dinner, there was time to make him standard corn bread. Corn bread is fluffier than corn cakes. Both versions suited Elvis, but only corn bread was served at dinner, usually with meat and vegetables. The buttery corn bread of Graceland was always baked in a blackened cast-iron skillet.

1 egg, lightly beaten
1 cup buttermilk
1 stick melted butter
1¼ cups cornmeal
¾ cup all-purpose flour
¼ cup sugar
2 teaspoons baking powder
½ teaspoon salt

Preheat the oven to 425°F. Grease a heavy iron skillet. In a medium bowl, stir together the egg, the buttermilk, and the melted butter. Place the dry ingredients in a large bowl and mix thoroughly. Stir the egg mixture into the dry ingredients until just mixed. Pour the batter into the skillet. Bake for about 20 minutes, until a tester inserted in the middle of the bread comes out clean and the bread is golden brown.

Yield: **1 skilletful**

"Just mix it" are Pauline's simple words of advice for preparing cornbread. "You gotta fix it real kind of soupy like. I would use a stick of butter to fix a skillet of bread."

Roast Beef

At Graceland, roast beef was always fixed in a skillet. The skillet was placed either in the oven or on the stovetop. Pauline preferred the oven method.

1 5-to-8-pound standing rib roast
2 garlic cloves, halved
1 teaspoon salt
½ teaspoon pepper
1 tablespoon vegetable oil
3 medium onions, quartered

Preheat the oven to 300°F. Rub the roast with the garlic cloves and sprinkle with the salt and pepper. Heat the oil in a large, heavy, ovenproof skillet over high heat and brown the roast very lightly on all sides. Add the onions and cover with a large piece of aluminum foil. Roast 23 to 25 minutes per pound for well done. Let the roast sit for ten minutes before carving. Preslice into small pieces in the kitchen. ("I cut it up for him," Pauline adds. "I did that all the time.")

Pauline remembers, "If it was just a small roast, it might take three hours or more. Sometime it would be real thick, a real thick roast, and it would take longer."

At Graceland, roast beef was accompanied by green beans, black-eyed peas, and mashed potatoes.

Dinner Parties

If Elvis was dining with Priscilla, the two would eat in the formal dining room. The cook would prepare their plates in the kitchen. However, when the doctor (Dr. Nick) came by, it was enough of an occasion to hold a "dinner party."

For a dinner party, the cooks would carry the food in large bowls on platters and set it down in the dining room. "Everybody could just sit at the table and fix their own plate with whatever they wanted to."

Elvis, however, never served himself or cut his own food up; that job was left to Priscilla, who "fixed" his plate at these buffets, piling his plate high with food and then cutting it into tiny pieces.

At Graceland dinner parties, the table would be decorated with "some candles and that's about it," according to Pauline. "We'd have some cornbread, and we might just have some meat loaf."

Meat Loaf

Pauline remembers these meat loaf dinner parties as follows: "We would have meat loaf (made with oatmeal) when a whole bunch of them were gonna be here. I'd just fix the loaf and put it on the table."

2 green peppers, diced
2 medium onions, diced
2 large eggs, lightly beaten
2 pounds ground chuck
1 pound bulk pork sausage meat
½ teaspoon salt
½ teaspoon black pepper
¼ teaspoon garlic powder
¼ teaspoon onion powder
1 cup rolled oats
1½ cups Hunt's ketchup

Preheat the oven to 350°F. Combine all of the ingredients except ½ cup of the ketchup in a large mixing bowl. Mix well and shape into a nice even loaf. Place the loaf in a shallow baking dish and top with the remaining ketchup. Bake for ninety minutes or until well done.

Yield: **8 to 10 servings**

Salad

Elvis' salad included whatever vegetables were in the Graceland refrigerator. On a good day, it consisted of:

Lettuce
Tomatoes
Radishes
Carrots
Cucumbers
Kraft Thousand Island dressing

Wash the produce, and slice, tear, or chop into pieces, as desired. Mix all ingredients. Add dressing to taste.

On a rare bad day, the salad was just lettuce and Thousand Island dressing.

Fruit Cocktail Salad

Elvis's favorite salad was fruit cocktail salad.

1 can Del Monte fruit cocktail
Raisins
Coconut flakes
Minimarshmallows

Open the can of fruit cocktail and pour it into a bowl. Add the raisins and the coconut and a generous portion of marshmallows. Serve chilled.

Beverages

Elvis' meals were accompanied by tea, coffee, lemonade, water (Mountain Valley Spring), or buttermilk. "How he loved his buttermilk," says Pauline. He always drank the Sealtest brand.

Elvis liked his coffee extra strong and served scalding hot. The Graceland kitchen used a Mr. Coffee to brew his java.

Iced Tea

"Ice tea was one of his favorite drinks," Pauline recalls. "Sweetened and strong. He didn't like no weak tea."

2 quarts water
12 Lipton tea bags
2 to 3 cups sugar

Pour the water into a kettle or a large saucepan and bring to a boil. Place the tea bags and the desired amount of sugar in a teapot or pitcher and pour the boiling water over the bags. Let steep for at least 5 minutes, stirring to dissolve the sugar.

Pauline remembers, "Oh boy, sometimes we used to use three cups of sugar for Elvis' tea. He wanted it real sweet. And then sometimes we would just sweeten some of the tea and then for the other we'd put some Sweet 'n Low on the table. If Miss Priscilla was there, she liked Sweet 'n Low. She didn't like the sugar."

Food for Road Trips

When Elvis went from Memphis to L.A., he took his bus, driving it himself. The kitchen cooked him a lot of food to take on the road. (He stored the food on board in a refrigerator.) Elvis always requested pork chops and sausage burgers for the long drive.

Barbecued Pork Chops

"I used to do a lot of pork chops for the bus trips," Pauline reminisces. "I would just season it, put in some barbecue sauce, and put it in one of those big ole skillets, and fix it in the oven."

2 large pork chops (rib or loin, cut 1 inch thick)
1 teaspoon vegetable oil
1½ cups Heinz or Hunt's barbecue sauce
¼ teaspoon salt
¼ teaspoon pepper

Preheat the oven to 350°F. Brush a heavy skillet with oil and place it over high heat. Brown the chops about 2 to 3 minutes per side and pour the barbecue sauce over them. Sprinkle with salt and pepper and place in oven. Cook 50 to 60 minutes or until chops are well done.

Yield: **1 to 2 servings**

Pauline wrapped the chops in tin foil to store them for the trip.

Sausage Burgers

"When they were fixing to leave," Pauline says, "I always mixed some big patties out of sausage like hamburger and cooked them up for him. That way they could have that for breakfast."

1 pound bulk pork sausage meat

Form sausage into 4 patties about ½ inch thick. Place in a large skillet and fry over moderately high heat until browned and cooked through, about 15 minutes. Wrap tightly in foil for a breakfast on the go.

Yield: **4 servings**

Hamburgers

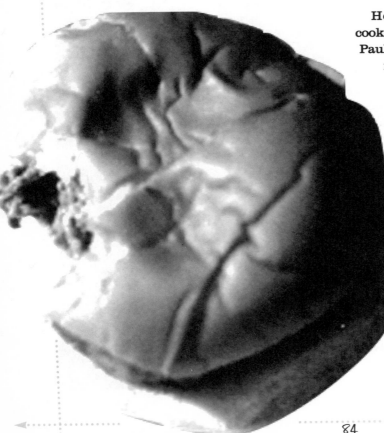

How did Elvis like his hamburgers cooked? "Everything had to be well done," Pauline insists. "Everything, his eggs, his meat, his rolls, and his hamburgers."

Elvis' hamburgers were not especially huge. They were only a bit thicker than frozen store-bought burgers. However, Elvis rarely limited himself to a single burger at a sitting.

Pauline made them up from packages of hamburger meat. She stored them in the freezer, popping them out as needed.

2 frozen hamburger patties

Fry the patties in a hot, ungreased skillet. Brown on both sides. Serve on commercial hamburger buns, with ketchup or onion gravy.

Fries

Elvis ordered two types of fries, "round" and "regular." "Round" are made from potatoes cut across, like potato chips. "Regular" are made from potatoes sliced lengthwise. Elvis told the kitchen ahead of time which type he wanted.

3 pounds russet or all-purpose potatoes
Mazola, Crisco, or Wesson oil for deep frying
Salt
Ketchup

Wash the potatoes well, and peel them if desired. Slice the potatoes thinly across for "round." Slice them lengthwise, about ¼ inch thick, for "regular." Keep the slices covered with cold water in a bowl until you are ready to fry them. Preheat the oven to 300°F. Heat the oil in a deep kettle to 375°F. Pat the potatoes dry with paper towels and fry ¼ of the potatoes at a time. Round should take about 1 to 2 minutes, or until browned and crisp. Regular should take about 7 to 8 minutes and be crisp and brown on the outside and soft on the inside. Sprinkle with salt and place each batch in the oven while cooking the remaining potatoes. Serve with ketchup.

Yield: **4 servings**

Pauline explains she "can't hardly tell which type he liked more 'cause he liked both of them."

Ham

On New Year's, Elvis had sliced ham, and black-eyed peas too. Peas on New Year's are an old Southern tradition for good luck. The cooks at Graceland didn't cure the ham themselves; they relied on cured smoked hams bought at the supermarket. Any brand would do as long as the ham was large. They then sliced it and fried it up. Pauline says the slices for Elvis "wouldn't be a half inch, not any more than a half inch."

2 teaspoons Mazola oil
1½-inch-thick slice cured smoked ham
¼ cup packed dark brown sugar
Pinch ground cloves
½ cup pineapple juice

Pour the oil into a large heavy skillet over medium-high heat. Add the ham slice and brown well on both sides, about 5 minutes per side. Combine the brown sugar, the cloves, and the pineapple juice in a small bowl and mix well. Pour this liquid over the ham slice and cook 5 or more minutes until a glaze forms.

Yield: **1 serving**

Black-Eyed Peas

Follow directions for Crowder Peas, page 79.

Candied Yams

The ham was occasionally served with candied yams. Pauline admits, "he didn't care that much about them." Here's the recipe, anyway.

4 medium sweet potatoes or yams, peeled and halved
¼ cup unsalted butter
½ cup packed dark brown sugar
1 teaspoon vanilla extract or ¼ cup lemonade (optional)
¼ cup water (optional)

Parboil the potatoes for about 20 minutes and drain. Combine the butter, the sugar, and the vanilla or lemonade in a large skillet. (Add ¼ cup water if using vanilla.) Stir over low heat until the sugar is dissolved. Add the potatoes and simmer, uncovered, stirring occasionally, until the potatoes are cooked and glazed, about 15 minutes.

Yield: 4 servings

Dessert

Sometimes Pauline had to make two or three desserts in one night.

"Elvis might want a cake, or potato pie, and then way later he might want some banana pudding. Now he loved banana pudding. For a while I always had to keep some banana pudding."

Banana Pudding

The banana pudding Pauline made was an adaption of the classic 'Nilla Wafer recipe. Here is the recipe found on the side of the Nabisco 'Nilla Wafers box.

¾ cup granulated sugar
⅓ cup all-purpose flour
Dash salt
4 eggs, separated, at room temperature
2 cups milk
½ teaspoon vanilla extract
35 to 45 'Nilla Wafers
5 to 6 medium-size fully ripe bananas, sliced

Combine ½ cup of the sugar, the flour, and the salt in the top of a double boiler. Stir in the egg yolks and milk; blend well. Cook, uncovered, over boiling water, stirring constantly until thickened. *(Per Pauline, "It gets real thick, thick like some buttermilk. Once you shake buttermilk up, its much thicker than sweet milk.") Reduce the heat, stirring occasionally for 5 more minutes. Remove from the heat and add vanilla. (Pauline says of the process, "It takes a long time to cook, real long, and you have to stand right there with it and keep it stirred cause it's so easy to scorch.")*

Take a shallow 2-inch Pyrex dish and cover the bottom with wafers. Stand some up all around the sides, too. Add a layer of bananas, sliced to medium thickness—not too thin, and not in big chunks. Cover with another layer of wafers. Pour on the pudding mixture. (For a time, at Graceland they separated the egg whites from the yolks and made a meringue to pour on top.) Let set, and serve chilled.

Cakes

At Graceland, the cakes were made from prepackaged mix, what they called box cake—Betty Crocker, Duncan Hines, or Pillsbury vanilla. Creativity was reserved for the icing.

Caramel Cake

To make Caramel Cake the way Pauline made it for Elvis at Graceland, ice a vanilla cake with caramel before it has fin-ished baking. You can buy the caramel icing already pre-pared, although Pauline made it from scratch.

1 medium box vanilla cake mix
1 can Carnation milk (12 ounces)
2 cups sugar

Prepare the cake mix according to package directions in a bundt pan. Fifteen minutes before the cake is fin-ished baking, mix the milk and sugar in a large skillet over high heat. Stir to dissolve the sugar and bring to a boil. Remove the cake from the oven when only 10 minutes are left, and slowly pour the syrup over the cake. Return the cake to the oven and let it bake another 8 to 10 minutes.

Pauline says, "While you're baking your cake, you still got to get your icing on. It takes a long time, cause it's gotta cook now and get real thick."

Pineapple Cake

2 20-ounce cans crushed pineapple
½ cup sugar
3 tablespoons unsalted butter
1 18¼-ounce white cake mix (Duncan Hines or Pillsbury)

Prepare the cake mix according to package directions and cool after baking. Drain and reserve the pineapple juice. Place the reserved pineapple juice, the sugar, and the butter in a 2½-quart saucepan over high heat. Bring to a boil, then immediately reduce to a simmer and cook for 20 minutes, until the mixture is thick and the consistency of icing. Mix in the crushed pineapple and spread on the cooled cake.

Yield: **1 cake**

For Elvis (and for herself), Pauline liked "adding a little bit of butter in the icing. I'm a butter fan. I got to be a butter fan after he got hot about butter."

Sweet Potato Pie

The sweet potato pies Pauline made at Graceland had white potatoes in them, her secret for lightening the color and heaviness of the pie.

Pauline made sweet potato pies on an industrial scale—"when I make potato pie, I don't wanna make just two or three," she says. She boiled so many potatoes at once that she needed to use a "huge roast pan, the black one with the white dots on it." Here are directions for a single pie.

2 small sweet potatoes, scrubbed well (about ¾ pound)
1 medium russet baking potato, scrubbed well
1 stick (8 tablespoons) unsalted butter, cut into 8 pieces and softened
1 cup packed brown sugar
½ teaspoon freshly grated nutmeg
3 large eggs, beaten
1¼ cups evaporated milk
½ teaspoon vanilla extract
1 9- or 10-inch unbaked pie crust

Preheat oven to 450° F. Place all of the potatoes in a 2- or 3-quart saucepan. Cover with cold water and bring to a boil over high heat. Reduce the heat to a simmer and cook the potatoes until they are very soft, about 20 to 30 minutes. Drain and, when cooled enough to handle, peel the potatoes. In a medium bowl combine the potatoes, the butter, the brown sugar, and the nutmeg. Using a potato masher, cream the potatoes until smooth.

In a small bowl, beat the eggs, 1 cup of the milk, and the vanilla together. Beat this into the potato mixture until thoroughly mixed. Pour the filling into a prepared pie crust and drizzle the remaining milk on top. Bake 15 minutes and turn oven down to 325°F. Bake for another 30 minutes or longer, or until filling is set.

Pie Crust

The pie crusts were made from scratch at Graceland. There was no sugar in the dough because the filling was so sweet.

When Pauline gets ready to make the crust, she "sifts the flour, gets some ice water, gets the Crisco. I work that Crisco in real well and then drop in the ice water, real cold ice water."

2 cups all-purpose flour
½ teaspoon salt
⅔ cup Crisco
4 to 5 tablespoons ice water

Sift the flour with the salt. With two knives or a pastry cutter, work the Crisco in until the mixture resembles crumbs. Sprinkle in the ice water, stirring with a fork until the mixture will hold together. Shape it into a ball and then flatten it into a circle to roll the dough out. Fit the rolled-out dough into a lightly greased 9- or 10-inch glass baking dish. Keep chilled until ready to fill.

Yield: **1 pie crust**

The potato pies were timed so that they were set out to cool while Elvis was at the movies. When he came back, they were ready to eat. He would drink glasses of ice water with the pies.

E lvis' snacks usually consisted of packaged foods—chips or candy bars. Packaged snacks are the universal food of America. They can be purchased virtually anywhere, in all regions, at all times, in the same wrapping, and at nearly the exact same price. They are thus the most democratic of foods, and not just because they are so cheap. Fritos, for instance, whether eaten by Elvis, the president, or a homeless person on the corner, are all exactly the same, crunchy and delicious.

These omnipresent packaged foods played a special role in Elvis' life. Given his origins, where virtually all foods were homemade, packaged foods in shiny wrappers represented the city and a larger world.

At the same time, Elvis had his own special tastes and pleasures, which went beyond mass market snacks. Who else but Elvis would be original enough to combine cheese and peanut butter on a sandwich?

Just as some people chain-smoke, Elvis chain-snacked. He didn't measure the quantity in packs, he measured it in cases—a case of yogurt, a case of Popsicles. Like a smoker, he was addicted.

Yogurt

For diet lunches, often aboard the plane to Vegas, Elvis would make do with yogurt. He would start with just one little plastic cup with a foil top, but by the end of the trip, he might have consumed a case. His favorite flavors were blueberry and peach, and Dannon was his favorite brand.

Popsicles

Linda Thompson, a former Miss Tennessee, introduced Elvis to the pleasures of Popsicles. Linda had a tremendous sweet tooth, according to Elvis' stepbrother, and she met her match in every way in Elvis. During Elvis' screenings at the Memphian, as he was busy sipping a large Coke and munching on a peanut butter cup, Linda couldn't help but fall in love with him.

Once he became a Popsicle freak, he could barely control his experimentation with various flavors. Banana, strawberry, grape, cherry—all had their day.

Elvis would send out Billy Stanley in the middle of the night to get them. Elvis would polish off the boxes of Popsicles as he lay in bed. In the morning, the maid had to clean up all the sticks.

Snow Cream

In the days before global warming, it used to snow in Memphis. Elvis would build a big fire outside Graceland. He and the guys would stay out in the snow till eight or nine in the morning, throwing snowballs at each other. And then (Elvis' favorite part of any blizzard) they would eat the snow itself, in the form of snow cream. Snow cream was made by mixing snow with vanilla extract and sugar.

As an accompaniment to the snow cream, Elvis sent out for burgers. These sometimes came from McDonald's or Burger King, but more often from a little place that Elvis' valet remembers as serving burgers that were like "little gut grenades, sort of like McDonald's, but deadlier."

Midnight Snacks

Even though Elvis could have food sent up to his bedroom, he enjoyed raiding the refrigerator. He enjoyed it so much, he had a refrigerator installed in his bedroom just to hold snacks.

Elvis had a mynah bird that lived in the kitchen. The mynah bird was trained to cuss. One night Elvis sneaked into the kitchen; he couldn't see the bird, which was black, in the darkness. As he opened the refrigerator door, the bird swore at him. Elvis thought there was somebody else in the room, and it scared him nearly to death. He calmed down only when the light from the refrigerator came on and he saw it was just the bird. Later he said he was "going to have that bird for lunch one day."

When he raided the refrigerator at night, Elvis principally liked fruit. The fridge was kept stocked for him with bananas, apples, grapefruit (for a while he had one every morning), cantaloupe, and watermelon.

Pickles

When he was recording, Elvis' favorite snack was dill pickles. A milk shake cup placed by his side was kept filled with them. Once, in Los Angeles, a studio musician tried to eat one. A member of Elvis' entourage rushed over before it was too late and stopped him cold: "No, no! Those are Elvis' pickles. Don't you touch them!"

Snacks for the Pool

Elvis enjoyed sitting around the pool eating watermelon hearts. For entertainment while he ate, he would float flashbulbs in the pool. Then he would take out a .22 and shoot at them. When they were hit, they would flash, and then sink to the bottom.

Snacks for Just Walking Around the House

As soon as Elvis walked into the house, he would turn on all the TV sets. Then, as he walked around the house, he would casually snack on Hostess Cupcakes, Eskimo Pies, Fudgesicles, Dreamsicles, and Nutty Buddies, either alone or all in combination.

Other days, he preferred hot dog rolls, plain, without the hot dogs. Elvis also liked Girl Scout cookies. And he loved Brownies best of all.

Milk and Bread

After breakfast, Elvis' favorite snack was milk and bread. Milk was buttermilk, and the bread, corn bread (see page 80). At Graceland, the maid said she always "buttered his corn cake on each side, like you would a pancake, before I served it to him 'cause he wanted his bread buttered."

Krispy Kreme Doughnuts

In the South, the words *Krispy Kreme* are synonymous with doughnuts. Krispy Kreme doughnut shops are a cheerful place to stop in many a Southern town, and Krispy Kreme displays in supermarkets, stocked fresh daily, are always a diverting sight for shoppers.

Elvis splurged on Krispy Kremes in a big way. He consumed about a box at a time. Jelly doughnuts were his favorite. They were purchased for him at the local Piggly Wiggly—Krispy Kreme didn't open a store in Memphis until after Elvis died. When they did open it, they built it near Graceland.

The Krispy Kreme corporation prides itself on how healthful its doughnuts are. "You'd have to eat sixty-four glazed doughnuts to get the amount of cholesterol in one egg," says "Mac" McAleer, the chairman of Krispy Kreme. At only 130 calories apiece, they are "one thing health-conscious consumers splurge on." There is a secret to Krispy Kreme doughnuts, a special ingredient that accounts for their crispiness: they're made from potato flour.

Elvis Cooks

Elvis only once cooked for himself. When he did, he invented a new dish. It was a late night at Graceland, and Elvis had made his way to the kitchen. Though hungry, he didn't call a cook. Instead, he prepared his own snack.

He began by generously spreading peanut butter on bread. Then, in a burst of creativity, he added a slice of American cheese. It was an Elvis original—a peanut butter and cheese sandwich. Perhaps he had to make it himself. No one else would combine the two ingredients. When asked why he did it, he replied, "Because I was hungry."

Peanut Butter and Cheese Sandwich (an Elvis invention)

2 scoops smooth peanut butter
1 slice white bread
1 slice American cheese

Slather the peanut butter on the bread. Add the cheese. Serve open-faced.

Elvis' Favorite Pizza

Elvis had cooks on duty around the clock and a private plane to fly him to any restaurant in the country. He could have eaten anything he wanted, from anywhere in the world. But what he craved most was pizza, made just up the road at Coletta's Italian Restaurant. Ensconced in Graceland, he sent out for several pies a week. But Elvis didn't just order regular pizza. He demanded a very special kind of pizza from Coletta's—barbecue pizza.

Coletta's Italian Restaurant is located on South Parkway in Memphis, just minutes from Graceland. With its checked tablecloths, comfortable family atmosphere, and convenient free parking, it resembles many other simple Italian restaurants serving robust homemade cuisine. But unlike these other Italian restaurants, Coletta's has made a contribution to both Italian and Southern cuisine: it is where barbecue pizza was invented.

Barbecue pizza is a cheese pizza topped with barbecued meat; barbecue sauce is substituted for the tomato sauce. Coletta's barbecues its own meat on an electric cooker and makes its topping from scratch. The coarsely chopped meat is generously layered over the cheese and is covered by a rich blanket of sauce. The assembled pizza is baked in the traditional way (rather than grilled, which would make it barbecued pizza). The cooking method is the only traditional thing about Coletta's pizza. Whereas many "designer" pizzas using nontraditional ingredients seem awkward or contrived, this is a pizza with presence. It is a whole new way to eat barbecue, and a pizza that sticks to your ribs.

Jerry Coletta, the proud proprietor and a seasoned restauranteur, tells the history of this consummate marriage of Southern and Italian food. Necessity was the mother of invention in this case.

Jerry explains: "Coletta's invented barbecue pizza in the 1950s. Coletta's was one of the first places in Memphis to have pizza, period. But people wouldn't eat it, it was too exotic for them. To get people interested in pizza, we had to add barbecue."

Elvis liked the pizza so much that he had a charge account at Coletta's. Colonel Parker received the bills. Elvis ordered in two or three pies at a time for a cozy dinner at home with Priscilla. 'Cilla had to pick them up. She would hop in her sports car and speed off to Coletta's, where the pies

Coletta's Barbecue Pizza.

seductively bubbled in their boxes, awaiting their trip to Graceland.

After his painful divorce from Priscilla, Elvis himself once set out for Coletta's. Instead of dining on the pizza at home with his memories of evenings with Priscilla, Elvis this time ate at the restaurant. He was accompanied by his entourage, including the deejay George Klein, who was himself a Coletta's regular. Rather than ordering the barbecue pizza with all of its associations, Elvis wanted to try Coletta's other specialty, ravioli. The ravioli was made specially by a woman every day but Sunday, and this was a Sunday. Elvis ordered the ravioli but they were out of it, so he had spaghetti instead.

Elvis never quite forgot those tender evenings when he and Priscilla shared Coletta's barbecue pizza.

Coletta's barbecue pizza has won many awards. It was featured at the famous Pizza Chef Showcase in Chicago, the Oscars of the pizza world. Once you've tried it, you'll know why it won so often, and why Elvis found it so appealing.

Coletta's Barbecue Pizza (Elvis' Favorite Pizza)

Dough
1 package (¼ ounce) active dry yeast
1 cup warm water (110°F.)
3½ cups all-purpose flour
1 teaspoon salt
¼ cup olive oil

Sauce
1 cup ketchup
⅓ cup tomato puree
½ cup tomato paste
1 tablespoon Worcestershire sauce
1 teaspoon white vinegar
3 whole cloves
⅓ cup sliced onions
⅛ teaspoon granulated garlic
2 teaspoons sugar
½ teaspoon salt
1 teaspoon dried basil
½ teaspoon black pepper
6 ounces water

Topping
2 cups barbecue sauce
12 ounces Wisconsin mozzarella (low-moisture, part-skim), shredded
2 ounces Wisconsin pasteurized process cheese, shredded
1¼ pounds barbecue meat (cooked and chopped pork shoulder), heated

To make the dough, dissolve the yeast in ¼ cup of the warm water and set aside. Combine the flour and the salt in a mixing bowl. Make a well in the center of the flour. Add the yeast mixture, the oil, and the remaining ¾ cup of water. Mix, stirring with a wooden spoon until a rough ball of dough forms and the dough cleans the side of the bowl. Turn the dough out of the bowl onto a lightly floured work surface. Knead the dough for 7 to 8 minutes until it is smooth and satiny (dust the dough with flour if it feels sticky). Dust a large mixing bowl lightly with flour. Place the dough in the bowl; cover with plastic wrap and a kitchen towel. Put the dough in a warm place to rise for 90 minutes until it doubles in bulk.

After the dough has risen, punch it down and turn it out of the bowl onto a lightly floured work surface. Knead gently for about 2 minutes. Roll or stretch the dough into a circle that is 16 inches in diameter and about ¼ inch thick. Place the dough in a 16-inch flat pizza pan. Cover the dough with a clean towel and let it rise a second time for about 45 minutes before adding toppings.

To make the Barbecue Sauce, combine all of the sauce ingredients in a 2-quart saucepan and bring them to a boil. Lower the heat and simmer for 20 minutes, stirring frequently. Remove the pan from the heat and strain out the cloves and onions. Let the strained sauce cool to room temperature, then refrigerate until ready to use. The sauce can be made one or two days ahead of time. (Makes 2 cups of sauce.)

To assemble the pizza, first preheat the oven to 500°F. Spread ⅔ cup of the barbecue sauce evenly over the dough to within ½ inch of the edge. Mix the shredded mozzarella and pasteurized process cheese and sprinkle them over the sauce. Bake the pizza in a hot oven for about 10 minutes, or until the crust is golden brown and the cheese is bubbly. Remove the pizza from the oven and spread the barbecue meat over the cheese. Warm the remaining barbecue sauce and pour evenly over the meat. Serve at once.

Recipe Source: **Coletta's Italian Restaurant and Wisconsin Milk Marketing Board**

Fool's Gold Loaf

The evening of February 1, 1976, found Elvis home at Graceland entertaining two favored guests in the jungle room. Capt. Jerry Kennedy was a member of the Denver police force, and Ron Pietrafeso was in charge of Colorado's Strike Force Against Crime. Elvis had met both men several years earlier during his period of extreme interest in law enforcement, which culminated in his surprise drop-in visit to President Nixon, who named Elvis a "special agent." Tonight, as Elvis sat on his Kon Tiki throne chair in front of the jungle room's babbling waterfall, the discussion centered on law enforcement in Colorado. Elvis, however, was reminded of something else. Colorado was the home of that absolutely delicious sandwich, the best Elvis had ever eaten: Fool's Gold.

Elvis had sampled the sandwich only once, when after a concert he was invited to a restaurant called the Colorado Gold Mine Company in the Denver suburb of Glendale. He ordered the house specialty, which was named Fool's Gold because of its outrageous price—$49.95. The first bite alone was enough to make a lasting impression on Elvis.

Now, months later, Elvis was reminded of those sandwiches. Both of his guests from Colorado were very curious about this extravagant treat. The King's policy when entertaining in his rock and roll palace was to grant his guests' every desire—your wish was literally the King's command, be it a game of racquetball at four in the morning or a down-home Southern breakfast at midnight. However, the "Fool's Gold Loaf," since it came from a restaurant in Denver, would stretch the limits of even Elvis' notion of hospitality.

Elvis gazed across at his guests, who were comfortably ensconced on the Hawaiian armchairs, cushioned by the rabbit's fur throw pillows. The conversation continued to revolve around the sandwiches. One of the guys impulsively remarked, "Boy, I wish I had me one of them now!" Elvis knew what he and his guests wanted and the thousand-mile journey to the Fool's Gold Loaf would not deter him. Elvis looked at his friends and shouted, "Let's go get 'em!"

Before the lawmen knew what was happening they were seated inside Elvis' stretch Mercedes along with another couple of Elvis' buddies, and whisked to the Memphis airport. Elvis' personal jet, the *Lisa Marie*, was waiting for them on the tarmac. As the four jet engines roared for takeoff, the excitement inside the plane revved even higher as Elvis and his guests were about to be flown the two hours to Denver for Elvis' favorite sandwich, the most mouthwatering sandwich known to the King.

Once aloft, Elvis, the lawmen, and the rest of the gang gathered in the plane's dining room, around its leather topped table with surrounding bucket seats upholstered in aquamarine plush. Though Elvis often snacked on the *Lisa Marie*, in anticipation of the filling treat to come his only indulgence was a bottle of his *vin de table*—regular Pepsi.

At the Colorado Gold Mine Company, the scene was frenzied. The call had come in from Memphis at midnight. The cooks had less than two hours to prepare the "takeout" order of their lifetime. The massive griddle was scrubbed clean in order to fry up the huge quantities of bacon required. The loaves of bread were quickly hollowed out and then briefly browned. The other ingredients were always ready. Miraculously, the staff completed its creation in the nick of time. The restauranteur, his wife, and a waiter sped off for the Denver airport with twenty-two loaves. As requested, a case of Perrier and a case of champagne accompanied the sandwiches, along with a chest of cracked ice.

Elvis' plane touched down at 1:40 A.M. at Stapleton Airport and taxied to a private hangar. The owner of the restaurant personally brought Elvis and his party the order on silver trays. For two hours in the Denver night, the feasting went on. It was typical of Elvis' generosity that he insisted that the plane's pilots, Milo High and Elwood Davis, join in the fun. Elvis, as usual, avoided the alcohol, instead washing

down the sandwiches with the Perrier. It was yet another night of dining Elvis style on food fit for the King.

And just what is "Fool's Gold Loaf"? Far be it from Elvis to settle for an ordinary peanut butter and jelly sandwich. Fool's Gold Loaf is a p.b.j. realized on such a heroic scale as to become truly Olympian.

An entire loaf of bread is warmed and then hollowed out. The sandwich is generously spread with peanut butter and an equally thick layer of jelly. Finally, lean bacon has to be cooked, at least a pound fried to crispness, to fill the remaining belly of the loaf. The massive loaf is then downed while the bacon is still hot. The serving size? One loaf per person. Here is our version.

Fool's Gold Loaf

2 tablespoons butter
1 loaf Italian white bread
1 pound lean bacon
1 large jar Skippy smooth peanut butter
1 large jar Smucker's grape jelly

Preheat the oven to 350°F. Spread the butter generously over all sides of the loaf. Place the bread on a baking sheet in the oven. Meanwhile, fry the bacon until it is crisp and drain it thoroughly on paper towels. Remove the loaf from the oven when it is evenly browned, after approximately 15 minutes. Slice the loaf lengthwise and hollow out the interior, leaving as much bread along the walls as desired. While the bacon is still warm, fill the insides of the loaf with peanut butter and jelly to taste. Arrange the bacon

slices inside the cavity, or, if desired, layer the bacon slices between the peanut butter and jelly. Close the loaf. Savor.
   Vegetarian variation: Omit the bacon.

Yield: 1 serving (Elvis), 8 to 10 servings (others)

Food That Put Elvis in the Mood

Food can put you in the mood. Food can seduce. As *Cosmopolitan* editor Helen Gurley Brown once wrote, "One appetite can feed the other in a never-ending cycle of sensation."

M. F. K. Fisher, the food writer, noted that bachelors in particular "use what tricks they have to make their little banquets lead as subtly as possible to the hoped-for bedding-down." Elvis' girlfriends certainly tried to seduce him through food; any girlfriend who could make a peanut butter and banana sandwich as good as his mother's always won a place in Elvis' heart.

However, food for Elvis was not merely an aphrodisiac or a means of seduction. Food played a more integral part in his sexuality. For Elvis, food didn't put him in the mood, food *was* the mood. Elvis incorporated food into the sex act itself.

The practice of using food as part of sex is called plating, so called because the erogenous areas are made into a "plate." After devouring what is on the plate you then devour the plate itself. There are many ways to fill up a plate. Fruit, first peeled, can be sliced and laid over the area. Whipped cream crowned with a cherry like a sundae can top it all off.

It was the 1970s, the time of the swinging single; plating was on the cutting edge, and Elvis, with his oral fixations, was a natural. In a bit of brotherly advice, he told his stepbrother that "it spiced things up." Elvis was able to do the two things he liked best at the same time. (Plating also eliminated the risk of pregnancy, and Elvis could avoid disclosing the fact he was uncircumcised.) His partners in the games were his more voracious girlfriends. Kiwis, grapes, and especially chocolate-covered cherries were his foods of choice.

Elvis preferred not to see his girlfriends totally nude—ideally they wore white panties. When the excitement grew too intense, he would peel off his girlfriend's delicate underwear with one deft stroke, revealing a tempting area covered with a frosting of whipped cream. A strategically positioned chocolate-covered cherry completed the buffet. Elvis then tenderly cleared the plate, down to the last morsel.

1 or 2 plates
2 kiwis, peeled (slicing optional)
1 can whipped cream
1 chocolate-covered cherry

ROOM SERVICE MENU

Room Service available from our Bar at any hour without service charge

24 HOUR SERVICE

ALADDIN HOTEL AND CASINO

7 Room Service with Elvis' Valet

Elvis' stepbrother Billy Stanley was the King's valet. He was responsible for ordering all of Elvis' food on the road as well as overseeing many of his meals at Graceland. After Elvis died, Billy went through some hard times but has recently turned his life around. (Billy's mother, Dee, married Vernon Presley in 1960.)

I met with Billy and his attractive girlfriend, Charlou, at my hotel suite in Nashville. Billy, who appears to be in his mid-thirties, has long curly hair and was dressed from head to toe in denim.

"I worked for Elvis six years on and off again and I'd get fired for various reasons," Billy told me as he lounged in front of the room's TV. "I remember Elvis had already eaten one pizza and was starting on another and I said, 'Where you gonna put it?' 'You're outta here.' He fired me

Billy Stanley caught eating a burger.

for it. But I ordered all his food and made sure it was cooked the way he liked it, so I had to talk to the chefs and stuff to make sure they were gonna be on twenty-four hours a day."

"Was this is in Graceland or on the road?" I asked.

"On the road, and there was always cooks in Graceland, you know, chefs."

"On the road, would you let room service serve Elvis?"

"No, I served the food. Usually there would be like a suite. They would bring it up the service entrance and I would take it from there and take a nibble or something like that."

I wondered aloud if Billy tasted the food first because there was a risk someone was trying to . . . to— "No, we never worried about that," Billy said, cutting me off.

I told Billy that I heard from someone at Graceland that Elvis used to eat primarily in bed. Billy confirmed this. "I'd

say on the road it was about seventy-five percent of the time he was in bed."

"Was it also true that Elvis never really drank liquor, or at least not very often?"

"He did it a couple of times just to see what it was like to be drunk and when he did it it was always margaritas or screwdrivers . . . He didn't like the feeling. I remember he got drunk one time and he said, 'I don't like this stuff.' He'd been drinking peach schnapps. He loved peaches. He'd just get on a kick. Very excessive . . . it wasn't no just sitting down eating a cheeseburger," Billy said. "Elvis was eating three or four. Banana splits and milk shakes to go with it. All at once. Breakfast, he always ate a couple of Spanish omelets unless he was at Graceland. Then it'd be some hard-boiled eggs or maybe scrambled eggs, a pound of bacon, biscuits and gravy, orange juice."

"Why wouldn't he eat Spanish omelets at Graceland?"

"They didn't really know how to make salsa that well—Charlou here makes a great salsa—they really didn't know how to make it. They're from the South, they don't know anything about Mexican food."

Would he eat the same sort of food in Vegas? "It just depends on how long the flight we had was," Billy told me. "Usually all of our flights went over two to three hours. And he would eat before we left or he'd have something once we got there. He'd usually eat right before he'd go to bed. That was usually every night, after the show. He'd kind of give me a look and I knew it was time that he was going to bed so I'd go order the food."

I asked Billy what Elvis wanted for

dinner. "I knew what he wanted," replied Billy. "It was no problem. I mean, it was very basic, unless he wanted a pizza or something, or he'd say cheeseburger delight. Cheeseburgers. That's basically what he ate eighty percent of the time. American. Well done, burnt, black."

"Anything on them?" I inquired.

"Well it depends, if a new girlfriend was there, no onions. A new face in the crowd, there was just no onions."

I paused for a moment to picture Elvis snacking with his date, and then I continued to grill Billy: "I heard somewhere he'd eat hot dog rolls plain. Without the hot dogs."

"Oh, he would eat hot dog rolls just walking around the house munching," Billy explained. "At Graceland, or L.A., or wherever we'd be."

"He'd just walk around eating?"

"Yea, and oh, he liked the Colonel's chicken too."

"Is that a pun?"

"Some people would take it as that," Billy snapped. "But I don't even think of that [expletive] when I say 'the Colonel's chicken.'"

This discussion of the Colonel's chicken raised the issue of whether Elvis went out to restaurants. "Well, sometimes, like I said, we'd go out to Colonel Sanders," Billy remembered. "Also, there was a hamburger place that a friend of mine owned. We was coming back from the ranch one time [the Circle "G" in Mississippi]. It was just a hamburger stand, and it was the first time I'd ever see him go into a public restaurant, except it wasn't really a restaurant. It was just a hamburger stand like McDonald's and stuff like that. He just went in there and all of us that were authorized just went in there with him and ordered three burgers and chocolate milk shakes, two orders of fries, and some guy was in there trying to start some trouble and Elvis ran him off. He was trying to start a fight with the manager. He was drunk and obnoxious and Elvis went over to him. You couldn't hear what he said. He just kind of whispered in the guy's ear and the guy just looked at Elvis and then walked out the door. The manager come over and shook Elvis' hand and said, 'Hey, the food's on the house.'"

Billy leaned back in his chair and relaxed after recounting this tale of Elvis' heroism. I kept focusing on the food—"What would the cooks cook for Elvis at Graceland?"

Billy, with his perfect memory, responded without pausing: "The only food he'd eat from them would be pork chops, mashed potatoes, green beans, black-eye peas, onions. Southern food. That's what they fixed him. And carrot cake." Billy licked his lips, and continued. "For ribs we would go out. There was a place called the Rendezvous. In Memphis. They've got the best ribs in the world. And we'd go there. Sometimes we'd take them to the theater. At night he'd rent the theater out. There was one guy that worked for him. We called him 'Hamburger James' 'cause Elvis would sometimes be sitting there and he felt like eating hamburgers and he'd say 'Hamburger, James,' and that was his cue to get a hamburger and he got stuck with the name 'Hamburger James.'"

"Did Elvis ever eat real rural Southern food," I questioned Billy, "like squirrel or possum?"

"He said he ate a lot of crow," Billy fired back. "No, once he got famous, he didn't eat any of that. Well, he liked turnip greens. Corn on the cob. They had poke salad when they were growing up. Tony Joe White had a song called 'Poke Salad Annie.' It's this little thing. It's a little weed-looking thing that grows out there. Looks like a little turtle green. You boil it for several hours and eat it."

It sounded more slimming than most things Elvis ate. I asked Billy if the cooks ever made Elvis special diet food. He continued to respond with rapt attention. "Well," reminisced Billy, "they would hear stories from people that said Elvis needs to lose weight and things like that. And he would call down and say, 'Come on sweetheart, I'm starving, I need something really good to eat.' They'd fix him whatever he wanted. They would make up some of the pork chops that they do real good."

"Did you ever put him on a scale?" I asked.

"No," Billy said. "I mean I got fired when I said something. 'Where you gonna put it?' He fired me for it."

"Did he say anything?"

"When he turned forty he said, 'I'm fat, funky, and forty,' and that was about it. He was a man that just loved to eat. I mean he loved food. He was the slowest eater in the world. Now, we'd be sitting there, sometimes his breakfast would get cold. I'd have to order it again. The Spanish omelets. He talked so much, I mean, he'd just be sitting there talking. Rambling on about what's happening in the world today, and what he wanted to do at night."

"Like eating?" I suggested.

"It's just something he enjoyed doing," Billy said.

"It seems that everything he did, he did all the way. That's what I like about Elvis," I offered.

"He was excessive," Billy agreed. "We all are in certain ways. He was so . . . he didn't use napkins that much, he used towels. He'd say, 'Bring me a beach towel.' 'Cause he'd make a mess."

This last insight caused a lull in the conversation. "What do you and Charlou say about ordering a pizza?" Billy looked enthusiastic. Charlou, who had been pretty quiet, voiced no objections. I called room service and then the interview continued.

"What was Elvis' usual first course at a sit-down dinner?" I wanted to know.

Billy stared off at the blank TV screen as if trying to re-create the scene in his mind. "He'd have a salad; he didn't like rabbit food though, he said. He would eat it, but he'd go through it real fast so he could get to the real stuff."

"Which was?" I prompted Billy.

"Let's see, lots of things. Roast beef, turkey, mashed potatoes, cranberries, string beans. He loved string beans, and then he would eat several helpings of that, with big ole rolls, butter, big glass of milk; he loved milk."

I asked Billy what Elvis ate on holidays. "On New Year's Eve," Billy remembered, "there wasn't really a whole lot of eating for that; there was a whole lot of drinking."

"I thought he didn't drink much."

"It depends on who you talk to," Billy said.

"That's true," I agreed, "so, on New Year's he might—"

"I know he got hammered one time because we had to help him to the car. He was drinking champagne that night. We had six bottles. I was only sixteen at the time. He kept telling my ma, 'Oh Ma! Don't worry about it, these guys are gonna start drinking sooner or later, it's New Year's Eve.' He didn't care much for wine or anything. He hated beer. Anybody who wanted to drink a beer in front of him had to drink it out of a glass. He just didn't like the sight of a beer can or a beer bottle around him, and the only reason that being 'cause his mom drank a lot of beer. She died of cirrhosis of the liver. She'd be out in front of Graceland feeding chickens, throwing corn out there, drinking beer. She was very country."

I wondered what Elvis did for his birthday. Billy described the party: "He'd eat a slice of his cake, that's about it, or he'd have a slice in front of everybody and then bring the cake up to the room. So I'd take it up there to him. It was carrot cake that he liked the best or chocolate cake. He ate a lot of cake."

I told Billy I thought all this snacking might have made Elvis ill. "Yeah," Billy agreed. "I'd say the last year was probably the worst. He got up to two hundred fifty pounds. He'd sweat a lot."

We were interrupted by a knock on the door. It was room service, delivering the pizza with everything on it, plus a Diet Pepsi and a six-pack of beer. As we ate, the TV was on, showing cartoons. Billy drew a diagram of Graceland's kitchen and Charlou gave me her personal salsa recipe. I asked Charlou, who looks like a country and western star, if she was from Tennessee. It turned out she's from the Midwest but studied country and western in college.

The sight of the bubbling pizza in front of us dredged up another memory

from Billy. "Once, I knew he was on this diet, but he'd just call me into his room and say, 'Billy, I can't live on this stuff they feed me. I've gotta have some real food, either barbecue pizza or some hamburgers or something like that,' so I'd go get it for him."

Billy reached for a slice of the room service pizza in front of us. As Billy bit into a shrimp on top of the pizza, he remembered, "Elvis tried shrimp one time but he swore it off right away. It was in Vegas. He didn't even eat the shrimp, really. He picked it up and smelled it and said, 'No, I'm not gonna eat this.' . . . He didn't like escargot. I know that. We were in Lake Tahoe and I think it was my brother Rick put him up to it. He started looking at it. Playing with it with his fork. 'Man, I don't wanna eat something I could step on when I walk out the door,' he said."

While he chomped away, Billy looked at

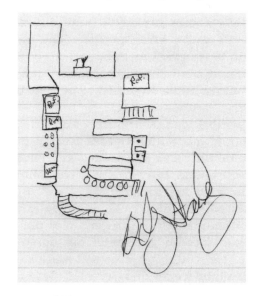

Billy's hand-rendered plan of Graceland's kitchen.

the cartoons on the TV even though the sound was off. I asked Billy if Elvis used to eat while watching TV. "Oh yeah! He did that all the time." Billy grinned. "There was a TV in every room. Even in the bathroom. He never ate while driving a car."

I continued: "Aside from drugs he took for medical reasons, were there certain drugs that gave Elvis the 'munchies'?"

Billy answered flatly, "I don't know about that. I know my experience when I was . . . when I . . . I'd just eat anything."

"Do you think that's why he was eating so much?" I pressed Billy.

"No, Elvis just loved to eat. Me, I'd eat everything, everything that he ate, but not as much. Some of it I still do. People can go the grave miserable if they want to but I'm not."

After hearing Billy's philosophy of food and life, I asked him if Elvis ever said anything along the same lines.

"Sure," Billy confirmed. "I mean, it's like he just couldn't survive on the rabbit food they were trying to push down on him. He said—what was it?—'The input has to be as great as the output.' By that he meant that given the energy that he put out, he needed the fuel to put out that energy."

Charlou looked on approvingly. Her appetite was evidently less hearty than mine or Billy's as she pecked at a slice of pizza. I asked Billy if Elvis ever shared foods with his girlfriends. "No," Billy answered. "He didn't like anybody eating off of his plate. He didn't share at all. 'I'll get you some if you want, but don't eat mine.' He wouldn't let me salt and pepper his food, he would do it himself. 'Get outta here, man, I can eat by myself,' he would say. He didn't like people going over-

board. There was a certain amount of kissin' up but not that far."

"You know how he used to give away cars and stuff," I reminded Billy. "Was he ever extravagant with food?"

Billy replied, "One year, everybody was expecting their Christmas bonus. He handed out these envelopes which held McDonald's coupons for cheeseburgers and fries. We thought that's all we were going to get . . . . He laughed about it real hard . . . then he gave everybody their bonus."

"What about at concerts? What would Elvis eat there?"

"We never had a bartender at any of our functions," Billy explained. "Backstage it was either myself or Charlie Hodge that served as bartender. We had some hors d'oeuvres and stuff like that. He liked these little finger sandwiches."

Charlou seemed interested in the concert aspect. "Did he have a rider?" she asked. "Did he have certain foods in his contract that had to be provided?"

Billy shook his head no. "But backstage there would be a party after the concert. He would be drinking water. There were guests, too. Gregory Peck, Rod Steiger, George Harrison, John Wayne. I think George Harrison had gin and tonic. I don't think he drank it, just held it in his hands. John Wayne had a beer. . . . Elvis used to sneak about ten of those finger sandwiches. He even put a couple in his pocket."

The few remaining slices of pizza lay in front of us. The grease had congealed. I asked more about the sandwiches Elvis used to stuff in his pocket: "Is that all he had for dinner?"

"If we were on the road," Billy said,

"these guys in Texas brought back some burritos after the show. And that's how he got into those. . . . I think it was a couple of policemen. Elvis was walking by. He said, 'What is that? Burritos? I'd like to have one of those.' So after the show, they brought a couple of burritos back there and he ate them. He ate them with his hands; he ate very, very slow." Billy said that this burrito craze lasted six months, and Elvis ate them "every day. Lunch and dinner. About three or four at a sitting. They tried to make them at Graceland, but burritos need salsa. See, that's where they got stuck. They tried to make salsa with some tomato juice and some hot stuff."

"They don't seem sophisticated," I said.

"Well, they're not as far as cooks go," he agreed. "If it's not Southern cooking, they'd take a stab at it. Elvis was into other types of foods, too. He picked up on fads before a lot of people got interested."

"I think Elvis was always on the cutting edge," I said.

"Crystals, you know, the rocks?"

"He was into crystals?"

"He had several," Billy said.

"Was he into health foods before most people?" I asked, though on second thought, this seemed unlikely. "I mean, didn't he eat a lot of fruit?"

"Every once in a while he experimented with some fruit in bed," Billy said. "What do you call those little things, kiwis? He and his girlfriend put kiwis on various parts of his body."

"Billy!" Charlou said.

"Which girlfriend did he do this with?" I was wondering if he meant Priscilla.

"I'm not going to say." Billy winked. "But he wasn't as kinky as everybody made him out to be. You know, these two-

way mirrors and stuff like that. There's a lot of things about Elvis that are misinterpreted or misquoted. He was basically just a normal guy."

"Very normal," I agreed. "He liked football, he liked hamburgers, he loved his daughter."

"He loved his daughter. He worshiped her. . . . He loved people and that's all there is to it. He loved life, he enjoyed every minute of it. Yeah, he loved food, people. Money wasn't a big problem to him. He never knew the value of the dollar, and thank God he taught me that, 'cause I can't stand people who live for the almighty dollar."

The interview was winding down. Billy and Charlou promised to call me when they were in New York (they told me they stay in the same building where Dolly Parton has an apartment). Downtown Nashville was deserted outside my hotel window. It was about four-thirty in the afternoon on a summer Sunday. I felt sick from spending the whole afternoon inside a hotel room eating pizza and drinking. I told this to Billy and we had one last exchange.

"Now you know how Elvis felt," Billy said. "He felt sick and thought, maybe if I eat something I'll feel a lot better. And of course, he'd been eating already."

I said, "I guess the problem was he couldn't go out. He couldn't go out into the city like we could."

"You've been cooped up in this room, right?"

"Yeah, I have."

"Well," Billy said, "now you've got the Elvis syndrome. You sit around a room, what are you gonna do? Start eating. That's why he did a lot of it. Boredom."

Elvis had always dreamed of being a movie star. "I don't know how long the music end of it will last," Elvis mistakenly said as he sought to switch the focus of his career to pictures. Elvis realized his dream and started an entire new genre of film in doing so: the Elvis Presley picture. These consistently upbeat movies were never well thought of by Elvis' fans, who perceptively sniffed out their exploitative nature and fraudulent tone. Elvis' biographer Albert Goldman, always critical, was even more dismissive. In his biography *Elvis*, he compared Elvis' movies to fast food: "The Presley picture [was] one of Hollywood's most stereotyped products: the entertainment world's equivalent of a franchise hamburger. Like the burger, the picture looked big and appetizing—until you got into it.

Then you realized that it was totally synthetic, devoid of any real satisfaction."

When Elvis arrived as a young man in the lotusland he had fantasized about, he found his life offscreen to be simple and bleak. He was a virtual shut-in in his eleventh floor suite at the Knickerbocker Hotel in downtown Hollywood. His nights never varied. He learned his lines, spoke on the phone to his family, and went to sleep. He took all his meals from room service.

As he grew older, however, Elvis fell in with the brat pack of his day: Natalie Wood, Sal Mineo, and Dennis Hopper. And he usually dated, or at least befriended, his leading ladies, among them Debra Paget and Barbara Eden. Elvis' dining habits also changed. He left his hotel room behind. Accompanied by his new entourage, Elvis ventured out, into Hollywood and the world of Hollywood restaurants.

Hollywood Dining

"Tinseltown is a mixture of the glamorous and the powerful and that's what makes the dining scene so interesting here," George Christy, the Hollywood gossip columnist, told me over lunch. "People love glamour and even the glamorous people like glamour so there are those that want to dine in a glamorous environment with glamorous people. There are a lot of powerful people here, and they do business in restaurants. Even if they're not known, there are a lot of beautiful young girls in Hollywood, a lot of handsome young men, and they

add a lift to any dining room, don't they? And since Elvis' day, our food has improved a lot."

To understand the food of Hollywood and the dining options available to Elvis, I had gone straight to George, a Hedda Hopper of our times; his column "The Great Life" in the *Hollywood Reporter* has a pronounced food focus, with restaurants often receiving as much attention as the celebrities interviewed in them. Not merely a critic, he has had several screen roles, including that of a terrorism expert in *Die Hard*. I interviewed George in Los Angeles at Madeo, an Italian restaurant filled with Hollywood executives and Hollywood wives. Amidst all the suits (on both sexes) George looked festive as he strolled in sporting pink pants, a pink shirt, and a matching pink sun hat ("Sunblock gives you skin cancer," says George, who kept on his hat throughout the meal).

As we ate a lavish antipasto assortment, I asked George what Hollywood dining was all about in Elvis' day, during the 1960s. "A lot of it was 'Hi hon,'" George promptly replied. "You know, the waitresses would all call you 'hon.' 'Do you want Roquefort on your salad?' they would say. 'We have such good Roquefort. You want a baked potato with your filet? We serve meat and potatoes and we have such good baked potatoes. Foil wrapped.' That was the kind of diet we had. And of course, we had surf and turf. Steak and lobster tail."

George then reminisced about the restaurants popular in Hollywood's glorious past, concentrating on the period Elvis was in town. "There were the little places that cropped up that were charming, a French restaurant called La Rue's. Nino and Bruno were the maître d's. A wonderful Italian restaurant called Patrone's in a little Spanish house and you could see Audrey Hepburn there, and Mitzi Gaynor. There were steak places like Sneaky Pete's that were popular. A place called Jack's at the beach. It was on a pier that was wonderful. I'm sorry that they've taken the pier down now. You'd see Fred Astaire or Gene Kelly there. The restaurant used to do their own guacamole. And there was Romanoff's. Run by Mike Romanoff. He called himself Prince. Of course, in Los Angeles you give yourself a title, and everyone falls for it, and that was very popular. It was comfortably continental. As was Chasen's. Chasen's of course has a great following. Dave Chasen—he's dead now. I was a pallbearer at his funeral. He was a friend of Harold Ross, of *The New Yorker*, who talked him into opening Dave's chili pit. Which became Chasen's. His widow, Maude, runs it now. Hitchcock dined there every Sunday night."

As George and I ate at Madeo, everyone in the room, including the actress Kelly LeBrock, tried to catch George's eye, but he was busy squirting more balsamic vinegar on his salad. I asked him about the social ambience that is part of Hollywood dining. "This is a working town, people don't stay out late, and people go to restaurants and do their work. There's that awful phrase 'power dining.' I hate it, just terrible. But there are a lot of powerful people here who wheel and deal all day; this is wheel-and-deal city. And they do business at breakfast, business at lunch, and business at dinner....

George Christy

If you go to the Ivy or Spago, people go there to see and be seen. To table-hop. As you see they do here too."

Elvis didn't table-hop. He had no need to see or be seen. Once, when he was dining at the restaurant La Scala on Santa Monica Boulevard, Elvis was approached by the maître d', who informed him that Paul Newman's kids would like to meet him. Elvis, who while shopping for guns had recently run into Newman, felt that Newman had snubbed him. Above all, Elvis was eating his dinner. His response to the maître d'? "Fuck Paul Newman and his kids."

At Madeo, there was a striking contrast between the plushness of the room and the restaurant's oddly casual touches (sodas were served in their cans). "Hollywood restaurants are informal," confirmed George, nibbling at his fruit tart. "They're relaxed. We're in a semitropical climate, and the weather dictates our life-style, doesn't it?... And when you see waiters in jeans. At the Ivy they're wearing white jeans, at Morton's they're wearing white jeans, at Spago they're wearing black jeans. That all kind of sets the tone, doesn't it?... And the restaurants allow someone in with a jacket and polo shirt. A lot of young actors will have a T-shirt and a jacket and I don't think they're gonna turn Warren Beatty away if he walks in wearing that." Elvis would have objected to the jeans. Though he was by no means a formal guy he never dressed plainly. He preferred ornate outfits. If Elvis appeared in jeans, it was only as part of a costume.

As our lunch drew to a close, I asked George if Hollywood dining had changed since Elvis' day. George replied, "I remember there was an Italian restaurant in the desert in Palm Springs like fifteen years ago. And the owner said he had to put 'Italian *and* American restaurant,' so that people wouldn't be frightened of just having Italian food." (Though "Hi hon" restaurants are still to be found in Los Angeles in the 1990s, rustic Italian food like that at Madeo's is possibly more popular than American or even Californian cuisine.) "We're more health conscious now, and we're more sophisticated," said George. "We're eating much more interesting food and the

Elvis in one of his celluloid food scenes.

food is much more sophisticated. It's become world-class cuisine.... People have traveled, they've tasted Italian food and Asian food, and they are not as frightened as they used to be of an odd taste."

Elvis Eats Out

This is the scene Elvis faced when he dined out in Tinseltown: table-hopping, a trend toward jeans, a growing influx of frightening foreign foods. All of this appalled Elvis. He went looking for another Gridiron Diner like the one back in Memphis. He brought Natalie Wood along on his quest. As they went from one hash house to the next, Natalie found Elvis' lack of sophistication fascinating. She once remarked about her dates with Elvis, "We'd go to P. C. Brown's and have hot fudge sundaes. We'd go to Hamburger Hamlet and have a burger and a Coke. He didn't drink. He didn't swear. He didn't even smoke! It was like having the date that I never ever had in high school. I thought it was really wild."

Later Elvis became too famous to go out at all. Though he was working in Hollywood, he was in no way part of the Hollywood dining scene. Ensconced in his house in Holmby Hills, he flew in chefs from Memphis, who prepared to his precise specifications his Southern favorites.

In L.A., Elvis wasn't the only star indulging in what could be termed "celebrity cuisine." It's an old Hollywood story for sudden fame to bring out idiosyncratic food habits in a star. Celebrity cuisine could mean ordering a chicken salad and demanding that the chef only

use meat from the left breast and a certain type of lettuce. Or it could mean ordering a chicken salad minus dressing and the chicken. However, brattiness or self-indulgence are only secondary characteristics of celebrity cuisine. The quintessence of celebrity cuisine is food geared to enhance the appearance, to promote the figure, hair, nails, and complexion of the diner.

Elvis cuisine shares certain traits with celebrity cuisine. It is very self-indulgent. However, it is in no way healthful or geared to benefit the looks (*au contraire*). And ultimately, it's much more democratic than celebrity cuisine. When he did go out, Elvis' favorite dining spot in Los Angeles was Tiny Naylor's, a fast-food chain in the Valley, where he would go, any chance he got, to grab a burger.

Food on the Set

Though Elvis was completely insulated from and indifferent to Hollywood restaurants, he partook by necessity of another type of Hollywood fare: the food on the set. "Catering" for Elvis meant catering *to* Elvis.

During filming of his first picture, *Love Me Tender* (20th Century–Fox, 1956) Elvis never ate in the Fox commissary. Colonel Parker set him up in a private dining room on the lot. All the other actors had an open invitation to join Elvis for lunch. Though they didn't necessarily like Elvis—they joked about his accent, his mascara, his blue suede shoes—they all showed up, because they could eat steak every day. However, it was no free lunch. The actors had to put up with the colonel, who always joined them, usually wearing

Barbara Eden

an old undershirt and ranting on about his "boy." At one point, the colonel pinned a pink "I love Elvis" button on Elvis' costar Bill Campbell. When Campbell tossed it off, the colonel looked surprised and responded, "We don't generally give away these big buttons." Elvis just kept on munching, no matter what was happening around him. While everyone else ate sirloins, he feasted on the usual delicacies: mashed potatoes with gravy and burnt bacon.

To find out what Elvis ate on location, I went to see Barbara Eden of "I Dream of Jeannie" fame. Barbara is best known to Elvis fans not for her TV work but as Elvis' costar in *Flaming Star* (20th Century–Fox). In this picture, Elvis played a half-breed who protects his Indian mother from white ranchers. Barbara was his love interest. It was

Elvis' most serious acting role; as Barbara put it, "Elvis didn't sing and he didn't get the girl [Barbara]." He wasn't going to dance, either, till it was refilmed to include a square-dancing scene. *Flaming Star* was one of Elvis' most critically acclaimed films, but it bombed at the box office. An interesting culinary point is that this movie was a western; instead of eating in a dining room on the lot, Elvis and his costars ate on the open range on food trucked in from the studio.

Today Barbara lives in a secluded canyon above Los Angeles. As with many of L.A.'s upscale neighborhoods, you wouldn't be able to tell the area was particularly rich unless someone told you how expensive the houses were or you noticed all the black Mercedes prowling around. Barbara's large ranch house had an American flag fluttering out front. When I met her, I first asked her what part of the city we were in. "90210," she sweetly replied.

Barbara looked sexy in black boots, tight black pants, and a black sweater. On her wrist was a glamorous diamond watch. We chatted in an airy pastel-colored room that overlooked a paddle tennis court in the backyard; beyond that you could see out over the green hills surrounding the lower part of the canyon. I sat nearly submerged amidst pillows covering a beige sofa as Barbara relaxed in a nearby armchair, a vast Lucite table in front of us.

I asked Barbara if Elvis ever talked about food. She answered thoughtfully and slowly, in an accent that was lady-like yet with a slight purr to it. "He did talk about it. He said he couldn't eat what he liked to eat because he had to diet. He was very concerned about gaining weight and said that it ran in the family and that he knew it. He watched himself and he loved Southern food, he said, but he couldn't always eat it.

"You look forward to a meal break on a movie. You're starving. It's so long, you know. By the time it's lunchtime you're ready to eat your hat....You're not treated like a star anytime you're doing a picture. It's a group effort. It's not a social thing. The only thing they do is they want the star players to get in line first because they want you to get in makeup early. So they will push you up in front, but that is only because it's expedient. They want you back on set in time. So we eat real fast and then we go back into makeup.

"We went out on location a lot so we ate whatever was on the wagon. The studio sent it out. On the wagon, or the truck as it is sometimes called, you could get beef, spaghetti, everything. Anything a restaurant would have. In the morning you could go and have burritos all the time. Eggs and chili and beans and burritos...for breakfast because you get there at six in the morning. You stay till the sun goes down.

Elvis lunching with Robert Wagner and a friend during the filming of *Love Me Tender*.

Elvis is the center of attention while he eats on the set.

"The stars served themselves. We all ate the same thing. I sat with Elvis all the time. We ate on the ground, and they had a table where you could pull up the chairs. And we talked.

"Elvis asked me a lot about my marriage. He spoke about marriage very much and was very concerned about it, and rightly so."

Was he "interested" in Barbara? "He was very interested in my marriage. He wasn't interested in me. Not really. We were friends. It was a comfortable situation. It wasn't a boy-girl thing at all."

I asked Barbara what the difference was between food on location and food in the commissary, and she told me: "When you're on the lot you part with your own money. When you're on location, they take care of it."

When Barbara ate on the lot, she dined separately from Elvis, who ate with his cousins. Barbara frequently dieted, subsisting on "a can of tuna and a hard-boiled egg." Elvis dieted, too. When Michael Curtiz, the director of *King Creole*, told Elvis during preproduction that he looked plump, Elvis promptly lost ten pounds in two weeks.

I asked Barbara if dieting alone kept her looking so good today. "I exercise, but not like Cher. I walk up and down the canyon. Two and a quarter miles in half an hour. I have to kick myself in the bottom to keep doing it, which is horribly human." While Barbara was saying this, she laughed and gave a familiar nod to her head. Though I had never met Barbara before, it was familiar because I thought Jeannie used to do it.

I asked her if this was Jeannie or Barbara speaking. "That was Barbara, that wasn't Jeannie," she said. "It could be Jeannie if you want."

I asked Barbara how she liked working with Elvis professionally. "He was wonderful. His acting talent surprised me. Elvis never seemed like a sophisticated star, even in later years. He was always an uncomplicated, kind, gentlemanly man. I would never say that he was naive. He wasn't naive. He was very smart. And aware of what was going on around him. He had good manners."

Did she mean good table manners? "Yes, good table manners. If he didn't [have good table manners] I would remember that. Manners are something you're either raised with or you're not. And I was. It's not an obsession, but your family either teaches you or it doesn't. You are what you are. It's like being born a blond or brunet."

Though I wondered what that really meant, I didn't interrupt as blond Barbara offered further insights about Elvis. She kept up with him after the movie, frequently seeing him in Vegas, where they were both working, Elvis at the Hilton, Barbara at the Riviera.

"Working in the concert field is a very lonely life. In that field all you have [to pass the time] is TV. In Vegas, you used to have four hours between shows. I played cards and read. If someone worked in Vegas all the time, like Elvis did, they were trapped.

"During the movie Elvis talked about why he watched a lot of TV, because he felt he couldn't go out in public, people wouldn't leave him alone. It's work, it's work to sign autographs and smile all the time; most people don't realize that."

After these lengthy reminiscences about Elvis and the hard work that accompanied fame, Barbara, gracious hostess that she was, now turned her attention to my comfort. We walked into her tiled kitchen, decorated with elephants and monkeys in a jungle motif, and she offered me a drink. Tab, she explained, was her favorite diet cola (she orders it specially because it's hard to find), and so Tab it was. Barbara poured it herself, squeezing in lemon to make it even better.

Energized by the Tab, I went on a tour of the house. We walked through large room after room, elephant motifs everywhere. "Elephants are my thing," Barbara explained.

During this tour, it occurred to me that Elvis was the sort of guy who would have loved to have a genie. I asked Barbara if Elvis liked the show. "Elvis was a 'Jeannie' fan," Barbara told me. "'Jeannie' has never been off the air. Elvis would enjoy the show." Then Barbara coyly stopped herself. "I won't tell you what he thought because it would sound self-serving. So I won't say what he thought of Jeannie!"

Soon we arrived in the library, which was filled with mementoes from her career. Unlike many of Elvis' costars, who are now dead or obscure, Barbara Eden is still working. Most recently, she hosted the 1991 Miss USA Pageant. And she's producing *I'll be There*, the sequel to *Beaches*.

On the wall were stills from Barbara's various movies. I looked for any reminders of Jeannie. Across the room, on a bookshelf, framed by racks of novels, I saw the bottle. It was nearly three feet tall and still iridescent. Though Barbara's house was lovely, this was Jeannie's home—she used to live inside.

Later, Barbara gave me a recipe for her favorite dip.

Barbara Eden's Dip (Lemon-Anchovy)

3 tablespoons Dijon mustard
2 egg yolks
Lemon juice
1 2-ounce can anchovies, undrained
1 shallot, minced
1½ tablespoons capers
1 cup corn oil
Dash of hot paprika
Pinch of salt
Freshly ground pepper to taste
¼ cup sour cream
Crudités

Combine the mustard, the egg yolks, the lemon juice, the anchovies, the minced shallot, and the capers in a food processor or blender. Process until smooth. While the machine is running, slowly add the oil. Fold in the seasonings and the sour cream. The dip is best after the flavors have blended, and the dip has been refrigerated at least two hours. Serve with mixed vegetables.

Yield: 1¼ cups

Elvis Films in Hawaii

Blue Hawaii was Elvis' most successful film, and the islands were the setting for many of those that followed. While making these films, Elvis fell in love with Hawaii. Hawaii was the most exotic place Elvis could visit without leaving the U.S. Hawaii had a regal tradition. Back at home, Elvis created the Polynesian-style jungle room at Graceland.

After finishing each film in Hawaii, Elvis often stayed on to unwind. A special attraction was the islands' tropical cuisine. Hawaiian cuisine for Elvis did not mean the real cuisine of the islands, which is a combination of indigenous, Japanese, Chinese, Filipino, and mainland U.S. influences. What Elvis liked was "Polynesian cuisine," the 1950s' ersatz exotica of pupu platters, colorful drinks with paper umbrellas in them, and artificial leis garlanding every neck.

Jane and Michael Stern's *Encyclopedia of Bad Taste* describes Polynesian food as "glowing with the lustrous hues of unadulterated food coloring...dizzyingly sweet and sour, fried and refried, soaked in coconut milk and larded with a sugary concentration of pineapples, bananas, and maraschino cherries."

Polynesian food became strikingly popular throughout the 1950s and early 1960s, when America was a sucker for familiar food in an exotic setting. Polynesian food was familiar. A luau was really just a backyard 1950s cookout. The only difference lay in the pineapple on the grill with steaks, as well as the aloha shirts and leis everyone was wearing, and the ukulele background music.

When Elvis went to Hawaii, he usually stayed at the Hilton Hawaiian Village in Waikiki, one of the most sumptuous hotels in Honolulu. The Hawaiian Village went all out for its luaus, which featured roasted pigs and Hawaiian music played by native musicians. It was all a little too authentic for the King, who mostly just watched the grass skirts on the waitresses. The only genuine Hawaiian food Elvis really went for was poi, because he could eat it with his hands. Elvis usually stuck to cheeseburgers.

In present-day Hawaii luaus are less common than before as they have been displaced by continental cuisine. The Hilton Hawaiian Village today offers a different kind of luau: a nouvelle "Kau Kau" luau. As Jeanne Datz, the Hilton's director of public relations, puts it, "We offer older recipes updated with a twist." The naive American cuisine of the 1950s has been replaced by authentic Hawaiian dishes reinterpreted for the 1990s.

The hotel calls it cuisine of the Hawaiian Islands and Flavors of the Pacific (courtesy Hilton Hawaiian Village Hotel).

Terrine of Molokai Vegetables Wrapped in Nori

5 ounces shiitake mushrooms
1 small shallot, peeled and minced
1 small garlic clove, minced
2½ pounds carrots
6 ounces daikon
½ pound asparagus
1½ pounds cauliflower
9 ounces boiling water
3 ounces powdered gelatin
6 ounces skim milk
2 sheets nori (dried seaweed paper)
4 fresh basil leaves
8 ounces fresh tomato vinaigrette
Sprig fresh basil
4 cherry tomatoes

Sauté the shiitake mushrooms with the shallot and garlic. Slice the carrots and daikon into long paper-thin strips. Cook in salted water until crunchy. Slice the asparagus tips and cook in salted water until crunchy. Boil down the cauliflower until it dissolves into a puree. Mix the hot water and the gelatin and bring to a boil. Stir in 3 ounces of gelatin water to the cauliflower puree, along with skim milk.

Take a terrine pan and line it with plastic wrap, making sure that you have enough wrap left hanging over the edge to cover the top of the terrine. Line the pan with alternating layers of carrots, daikon, asparagus, and mushrooms until the terrine pan is half-full. Pour the cauliflower puree into the terrine pan. Continue to alternate the layers of vegetables until the pan is full. Cover with the remaining plastic wrap and let it sit in a refrigerator overnight.

Take the terrine out of the pan and remove the plastic wrap. Lay the nori flat on a countertop and place the terrine on top. Roll the terrine up in the nori, similar to rolling a sushi roll. Dampen the edge of the nori to seal. Serve sliced with tomato vinaigrette. Garnish with fresh basil leaf and cherry tomatoes.

Yield: 4 servings

Brochette of Island Mahi Mahi and Kahuku Shrimp

Brochette
1 red bell pepper
1 green bell pepper
1 pound mahi mahi, cut into 12 cubes
8 Kahuku shrimp
4 cherry tomatoes

Brochette Sauce
2 cups fish stock
4 teaspoons soy sauce
2 teaspoons Dijon mustard

Prepare the red and green bell peppers by coring out their seeds and blanching them. Slice the peppers into the desired chunk size for the brochette. Alternate the mahi mahi, the bell peppers, and the shrimp on a skewer, and top the skewer off with a cherry tomato. Skewer the shrimp whole, two per skewer. Grill or barbecue to the desired doneness at medium-high heat. Serve with saffron rice or another desired starch, and garnish with grilled vegetables.

To make the sauce, simmer the fish stock over low heat. Stir in the soy sauce and the Dijon mustard while the sauce is simmering. Ladle some of the sauce on a plate to the side of the cooked brochette.

Yield: **4 servings**

Grilled Molokai Venison Sausage with Taro-Potato Pancakes

1 pound venison sausage
2 pounds shredded taro strips
1 pound shredded potato
2 ounces chopped onion
1 teaspoon sesame oil
2 raw eggs, scrambled
1 teaspoon tempura batter
Salt and pepper to taste
1 tablespoon vegetable oil
2 cups brown gravy

Blanch the sausage and then slice it in half horizontally and cut it into approximately 16 pieces. Broil the sausage on both sides. Serve with taro-potato pancakes and brown gravy.

To make the taro-potato pancakes, steam the shredded taro and potato for 1 minute (this helps bind the taro and potato together). Mix in the chopped onion, the sesame oil, the egg, and the tempura batter. Add salt and pepper to taste. Add the vegetable oil to a frying pan and place over medium heat. Pat the taro-potato mixture into small pancakes (about 3 ounces each) and fry on both sides until golden brown.

Yield: **4 servings**

Food on Film

In the title scene of *Clambake* (United Artists, 1967) Elvis tosses plastic-looking barbecued chicken carcasses to dancing chorus girls on a beach. He sings, "Mama's little baby loves clambakes," to the tune of "Mama's little baby loves shortcakes, shortcakes." Flaming shish kebabs are carried past, and a chef shakes a cocktail jigger to Elvis' beat as he stands over a buffet of clams and a large bowl of Jell-O. In real life Elvis didn't like clambakes; he didn't eat mollusks. However, the food Elvis enjoyed offscreen was often just an imitation, and an imperfect one at that, of the "hyperreal" Technicolor food served onscreen. No burger in real life could look as good as the prop burgers in his films.

In various scenes in *Clambake* (which is nominally set in Miami), the viewer is presented with images of fountains spouting pink champagne with a cigarette girl marching in front; a "Moorish restaurant" decorated with plastic grapes where the waitresses are dressed as harem girls; and a buffet consisting of a bed of ice sprouting toothpicks like a porcupine, each pick embedded with an olive. The food in the film is naive, opulent, and optimistic. This period quality was very Elvis. Like his films, essentially fantasy travelogues for couch potato fans, Elvis cuisine was a fantasy creation that was very much of its time. The films showed how people could live and eat if they just had the money, and Elvis had the money. The setting for his meals in real life—Las Vegas, Hawaii, or the jungle room at Graceland—came straight out of the movies.

In *Blue Hawaii* Elvis plays the son of a pineapple planter who wishes to leave the family plantation to become a tour guide and work with the girl he loves. His mother, Sarah Lee (Angela Lansbury), and Japanese houseboy, Ping Pong, try to keep him at home by serving him lavish cakes and mai tais. Elvis turns down the mai tais in favor of pure pineapple juice, and marries his love. It's true that offscreen Elvis didn't drink alcohol, but he was hardly that clean-cut. He appears to be so listless throughout this creaky and pointless picture that it wouldn't be surprising to learn he had been downing handfuls of tranquilizers between takes just to get through it.

In the late 1960s Elvis' movies became increasingly sleazy and filled with double entendres. In *Girls! Girls! Girls!*, in the Chinese meal sequence, a Chinese couple says, "Chinese meal is like a date: after you have one, an hour later you want another." Meanwhile, Elvis' girlfriend seductively eats a shrimp, anticipating Jennifer Beals' lobster scene in *Flashdance* by several decades. Elvis was disgusted by the smut in his pictures. Offscreen, he used food in his sexuality in a much more explicit way. Yet all the food-sex jokes in the film showed to Elvis just how low-class his pictures had become. Elvis had had enough. He had originally come to Hollywood to became a great movie star. In his later years, however, surrounded by Southern foods from his youth, Elvis literally couldn't stomach his movies; watching them almost made him want to vomit. After 1969 he stopped making movies and applied his talents to Vegas. There were no more fantasy food scenes for Elvis on the screen.

9 Vegas  Cuisine

Like the cocktail waitresses clad in short tunics encrusted with rhinestones, like the delicate but intense neon signs of the strip, Vegas food is alluring, a glittering tease that sometimes delivers. Vegas dining can mean waiting in line for hours for an all-you-can-eat buffet only to find the selections consist of grungy dinerlike foods that you can't eat at all. But if you are a high roller, Vegas dining can mean a $4,000 breakfast of scrambled eggs, caviar, champagne, and scotch—complete with a massage by the waitress between courses.

More has been written about the architecture than the cuisine of America's greatest resort. In their book, *Learning from Las Vegas*, the architects Venturi, Brown, and Izenour study the iconography of the Las Vegas strip, "reading" the glittering signs as ornaments, symbols, and a system of communication. However, if they had literally read what is written on the signs, they would have discovered advertisements for food: "King Crab Legs, $9.99" it says at the Dunes; "Legs, Breasts, and Thighs, $3.95 all you can eat" touts the Marina. Food, as much as entertainment or architecture, makes the town roll; it is yet another currency of this desert oasis.

"People in Las Vegas like flashy, showy, tableside cooking," said Lloyd Wentzell, Food and Beverage Director at the Aladdin Hotel and Casino, the hotel where Elvis was married. "Las Vegas is more glitzy than elegant, and showy presentation is what people want." I was speaking with Lloyd in the Aladdin's executive offices deep in the bowels of the hotel. Lloyd, a dapper ex–New Yorker who previously worked at the Waldorf Astoria, described some of the food "amenities" he has created, gifts that go into high rollers' rooms. In his office he had samples of chocolate brandy snifters, some with the liquor already inside. Lloyd became excited as he described additional items his star guests could expect to receive: chocolate-dipped strawberries, chocolate truffles, cheeses, a "German platter" consisting of an assortment of beers. For Valentine's Day, Lloyd had created an edible chocolate jewelry box in the shape of a heart. The box is designed to nestle in the middle of a heart-shaped cake, creating a memorable edible proposal or gift.

Lloyd then took me behind the scenes

Elvis relaxing with Priscilla in Vegas.

and into the Aladdin's massive kitchen, where that special wedding meal for Elvis and Priscilla was prepared. We walked through numerous winding corridors around the casino and entered the kitchen area, where clouds of steam billowed. In one room I saw a three-feet-deep vat of bubbling chicken soup overflowing with whole chickens. At the center of the kitchen the shiny stainless steel food lines for the hotel's numerous restaurants lay empty as it was still a few hours till lunch. Several employees were busy polishing what looked like a hundred real silver teapots. A chef in an immaculate white hat strutted about in front of a huge grill that was larger than any in an Army mess. Lloyd regretted that I wouldn't be able to meet his seven Chinese chefs, who had the day off. He had flown them in from China to prepare the Aladdin's sumptuous Chinese buffet.

A hallmark of the cuisine prepared by this kitchen, and in all the kitchens of Vegas, is that it is very cheap. The Chinese buffet at the Aladdin is only $3.95 at lunch, $4.95 at dinner, all you can eat, desserts and beverages included. Underlying the inexpensive yet generous portions that typify Vegas cuisine are some very unusual economics.

Lloyd told me, "I lose money every time somebody walks into that buffet." The $4,000 dollar caviar-and-scotch breakfasts are a loss to the hotel as well, for any gambler who is anyone is R. F. & B—room, food, and beverage comped. F. & B. is a loss leader in Las Vegas. The casinos don't expect to make money on F. and B., unlike in Atlantic City where the meals are seen as a source of income. In Las Vegas, revenue comes from gaming. The dining tables are just a lure to the gaming tables. (Additionally, free drinks are always available at the gaming tables as an inducement to lavish spending.) The food of Vegas, in Lloyd's words, "is merely designed to attract people into the hotel. And a certain percentage will play slot machines or play table games, and it creates activity."

The casinos calculate these percentages with the same skill with which they calculate the odds on gambling, and like all games of "chance" in Vegas, the odds are always in the casino's favor. Marketing departments track the correlation between how the buffet did on a particular day and how the casino did, and make appropriate adjustments in menu, marketing, and price. Similarly, for those players who are R. F. & B., the casino does a careful calculation determining a gambler's "rate" by the amount of money he plays. Only the highest rollers "rate" a $4,000 breakfast.

Despite the cool pragmatism of the casino's food calculations, the resultant excess of Vegas cuisine has its own pleasures. The family of five at the $4.99 buffet—two fat parents and three fatter children—are in pig heaven as they find themselves in a place where they can stoke themselves past caring on food, food that underneath its flash is just a variation on the familiar industrial food from home. This pleasurable excess is what Elvis liked about Vegas. And Elvis played a role in Vegas equivalent to the extravagant buffets: An all-you-can-eat dinner with a continually replenished dessert table is a loss leader but a way to attract clientele. Elvis Presley, the planet's best known entertainer, was far more expensive than any cheesecake but he was also by far the biggest attraction in town.

Elvis in Vegas

Elvis, who is more closely identified with Vegas than anyone except perhaps Liberace, and of course, Wayne Newton, first blew into town in the spring 1956...and was blown right out again two weeks later. Elvis was playing the New Frontier as the star of a show also featuring the Freddie Martin Orchestra and comedian Shecky Greene. For two weeks the twenty-one-year-old rocker tried to entertain a middle-aged audience, and for two weeks they just didn't get it. Elvis saw his name go from top of the marquee to the bottom. *Newsweek* likened his presence among his co-stars to "a jug of corn liquor at a champagne party." Elvis did not appear again in Vegas for twelve years.

When Elvis did appear again, at the Showroom at the International (which later became the Hilton), the man who strutted onto that Vegas stage made even the neon skyline of Vegas look understated and drab. Elvis outshone the strip. Whereas years before the town wouldn't give Elvis the time of day, now all of Vegas was captivated by the King. People fought one another for the few available tickets because only a lucky few were admitted. Blocks of tickets had already been reserved for the record company list, hotel list, Colonel Parker's list, and Elvis' personal list. Looks were important too. Once the mayor of Las Vegas called the Hilton on behalf of the mayor of a California city who was calling on behalf of a female fan who wanted to sit right in the front row. Unfortunately, the fan could not be accommodated: She was homely. Elvis insisted that only pretty girls could sit in the front rows.

The King of Vegas.

Excitement in Vegas.

Elvis, during his Vegas period, dropped the leather-clad rockabilly look in favor of the grandiose image we now associate with the mature Elvis. Tightly laced into a corset and dressed in a white jumpsuit secured by a massive gold belt, Elvis displayed all the trappings of royalty. To the heraldic sounds of the 2001 theme, Elvis lurched on stage each evening in his massive jewel-encrusted cape, pearls swirling around his waist and neck. Muttonchop sideburns and studded bell-bottoms completed the look. Some nights the words were slurred, the body too large to be contained by the corsets as the flesh split open the costumes. Yet every night Elvis appeared onstage before a frenzied audience. And when he threw his sweat-dampened scarves to the women in the front, the room reached a feverish state of hysteria as audience members clawed one another for a relic of the King.

Massive intakes of food fueled this massive display of talent. After the show, Elvis might have a small backstage party, but more typically he would rush to the Hilton's service elevator to be whisked to his penthouse suite for dinner. These gargantuan dinners created the body which could barely squeeze into the costumes. The grandeur of these meals lay not in the ingredients or presentation but in their sheer bulk. Elvis had all the Hilton's food facilities at his disposal, including the hotel's international restaurants and lavish buffets. But Elvis never entered the restaurants. He lived on hamburgers and more hamburgers piled high, high across his bed.

Elvis' suite, the aptly named Imperial Suite at the Hilton, was the grandest in

Desserts of the Las Vegas Hilton.

Vegas, with four bedrooms, jacuzzi, kitchen, sauna, and an enormous sunken living room with a clear view of the surrounding mountains. When Elvis was in residence, the suite was "made up" to his specifications with the windows taped up to keep out any light. When Elvis returned to the suite after each show, he might talk to other entertainers or joke around with the security people until it was "that time." That time to Elvis and his staff meant dinner time (usually around 5:00 or 6:00 A.M.). Elvis merely had to glance at his valet, Billy Stanley, to notify him to clear out the suite and order the food. Unless Elvis specified pizza or some other exotica, he didn't have to say what he wanted, Billy knew what Elvis wanted: Cheeseburger Delight.

Once room service heard Billy's voice phoning in Elvis' order, they knew without asking how to cook the cheeseburgers: burnt. The Hilton is so large that room service has its own separate kitchen on the second floor where the meals are prepared; waiters rushed the burgers to Elvis' suite atop the hotel. Billy signed the checks and wheeled the cheeseburgers into Elvis' bedroom.

Elvis ate the cheeseburgers in bed. They were served with ketchup but without mayonnaise because Elvis believed mayo was bad for your stomach and your throat. Fries, with the occasional pickle, were the only accompaniment. In Las Vegas, Elvis never had dessert after dinner. Following or during dinner, with the burgers only partially eaten, Elvis would nod off. Another day of Vegas dining was over for Elvis.

Meanwhile, after Elvis' show was over, the crowd would disperse in search of their own dinners. Food was not served in the Hilton Showroom, so they had to look elsewhere. Some might stop first in the lounge for a drink, hoping to catch sight of Elvis. Bobbie Joe Ozuna was a cocktail waitress who worked the lounge during Elvis' Vegas days. Once, when Elvis came in with the Colonel, Bobbie Joe broke down into tears. Elvis thought she was weeping with emotion. Her contacts were bothering her. He sat next to her and tried to comfort her and calm her down. She kept crying because of the contacts, but she was nonetheless truly moved by his action.

Most audience members headed over to the strip. The best act in the history of Vegas called for the best dinner. All-you-can-eat all-night buffets were not for Elvis' opening night audience. They wanted something much more opulent and elegant. Nothing was more impressive to one's date than a dinner served flambéed (especially if it was comped). If the fans were lucky, they dined on the following two diverting dishes from the Aladdin, which exemplify better than any others the glamour and sizzle of Vegas cooking. These flammable favorites say high roller, they say suave, they say Vegas.

Steak Diane

1 8-ounce New York strip steak
Vegetable oil for frying
½ ounce chopped shallots
Crushed pepper
A-1 Sauce to taste
Dijon mustard
1 ounce medium sherry
1 teaspoon butter
Fresh chopped parsley
½ ounce cognac

Trim all fat off the steak. Set it on a piece of Saran Wrap. Set another piece of Saran Wrap on top and flatten the steak with a mallet. Make the steak real thin.

On a gridiron or the top of your stove heat a pan till it's very hot; add a few drops of oil. Set the steak in the pan for 10 seconds or so on each side. Remove and set the steak on a platter to the side. Add the chopped shallots, some crushed pepper and A-1 Sauce, a little Dijon mustard and the sherry to the pan. Cook for a few seconds, then add the butter, stirring to mix.

Put the steak back in the pan and sauté 2 seconds on each side. Remove to a serving plate and pour the sauce over it. Sprinkle with a little chopped parsley. Pour ½ ounce of cognac over it and flambé.

Yield: **1 serving**

Recipe Source: **Aladdin Hotel**

Crepes Suzette

12 eggs
3 pints milk
2 ounces sugar
Salt
1 pound all-purpose flour

Beat the eggs and the milk together for two minutes. Add sugar and salt. Add flour a little at a time, mixing after each addition. Let set overnight. Roll out thin crepes.

Sauce

4 ounces butter
4 ounces sugar
1 orange rind, grated
1 lemon rind, grated
Juice of 2 oranges
Juice of 1 lemon
1 ounce Grand Marnier
1 ounce cognac

In a pan on medium heat, melt the butter, and then add the sugar. Cook for just a few minutes and then add the orange and lemon rind. Cook a little longer. Add the orange and lemon juice. Bring to a boil.

Dip the crepes in the sauce and fold one at a time. Set on a plate. Warm up the Cognac and Grand Marnier in a pan and pour over the crepes. Light the crepes with a match.

Yield: **12 Crepes**
Recipe Source: **Aladdin Hotel**

Elvis' Wedding

It was a Vegas wedding for Elvis. Elvis and Priscilla were married at the Aladdin hotel, owned by the Colonel's friend Milton Prell. Milton was the front man for the Chicago mob. (The Aladdin has since changed ownership.) Elvis and Priscilla arrived for their wedding with their hair dyed identical shades of jet black. She had lined her eyes with the heaviest black Cleopatra-style makeup. Elvis beamed at his bride-to-be.

The ceremony was held in a normal motel room in the "Camelot" area at the back of the hotel rather than a reception room. Only a few friends were present. The couple exchanged vows in front of Judge Zenoff, another crony of the Colonel's. Priscilla changed her vows from "love, honor, and obey" to "love, honor, and comfort."

The small reception afterwards was an affair Elvis would never forget, or forgive. Although the hotel went all out, little appealed to Elvis' palate. A champagne breakfast featuring, among other dishes, Oysters Rockefeller, did nothing for the King. However, Elvis changed his tune when it came to the cake, which had six tiers and was decorated with pale pink hearts. Elvis and Priscilla, now husband and wife, cut the cake and then fed each other delicious slices. Beaming at his bride over their wedding cake, Elvis was more in love than he had ever been before or was ever to be again.

Elvis Presley's Wedding Cake

11 pounds Sweettex
20 pounds cake flour
28 pounds sugar
12 ounces salt
1 pound, 4 ounces baking powder
3 ounces cream of tartar
1 gallon milk
10 pounds dry milk
2 gallons egg whites
2 quarts whole eggs

Preheat the oven to 350° F. Cream Sweettex and cake flour for 5 minutes at a number 2 speed on a four-speed mixer. Add the next five ingredients. Cream up to 5 minutes at the same speed as before. Then add remaining milk, egg whites, and whole eggs in two parts. Cream up to 5 minutes at the same speed. Put into different size molds. Bake at 350°F. from 25 minutes to 40 minutes depending on the mold size.

Icing

8 pounds sweet butter
8 pounds cake shortening
25 pounds XXXX powdered sugar
2 quarts egg whites
Vanilla extract to taste
Red food coloring

Cream the butter, shortening, and sugar in mixer for 10 minutes, then add the egg whites.

Flavor to taste with vanilla. Cream another 10 minutes or longer to lighten. It is then ready to use. Take some icing aside and add drops of red food coloring until pink to create pink hearts for decoration.

Recipe Source: **Aladdin Hotel**

10 Love Me Slender:

The Elvis Diets

Elvis' weight was as volatile as a soufflé, rising and falling at the slightest change in his mood. He fought a weight problem his whole life, but what is remarkable is that even if he ultimately lost the war, he won many battles. Elvis was never really a "big person" until the end, when he weighed close to 250 pounds. Even then, "it wasn't really fat, I know that," says Elvis' stepbrother, Billy Stanley. "It was water retention."

Though Elvis sometimes gained fifty pounds between performances, until his final years, he was always able to miraculously slim down before appearing in public. His diet techniques were radical, but so were his results. How exactly did he do it?

Diet Pills

One Friday afternoon in 1959, Elvis, who was serving in the army in Germany, made a stop at the post's dispensary. On this particular Friday, he was giving his buddy Rex Mansfield a ride home and so the two went to the pill-filled dispensary together. As Elvis walked up to the counter, he turned to Rex, smiled, and said, "Rexadus, it ain't what you know but who you know that counts in this old world." Elvis told Rex quite a lot about the little pills, which he said were "appetite depressants." Elvis claimed they made a "person slim and trim."

Aerobics

Exercise is a necessary part of any effective diet program. Elvis believed in this maxim wholeheartedly. Personal experience had shown him that diet pills could only temporarily control his weight. Elvis, of course, never took an aerobics class, kicking and bouncing in shorts to disco. His physically demanding performances kept him thinner than any exercise plan could. He sweated so much that he needed several changes in costume and was rubbed down after each show like a boxer after a fight. Between shows, Elvis resorted to traditional workouts to keep thin. His exercise program was so successful that Elvis often had no need for dieting or diet pills. Here is what he did to stay in shape:

Karate

Although the craze swept the United States only in the 1970s, it had been part of Elvis' life since the army. He had begun training with Germany's top black belt, Herr Seydel, who taught him basic kicks, chops, and lunges. In the army, Elvis felt he needed someone to practice on, a karate "dummy." The job fell to poor Rex Mansfield. Rex had to endure various punches and jabs from Elvis in front of Elvis' family in Germany.

Elvis and his wife were both active in the karate world. (Priscilla trained with Chuck Norris.) Elvis took her to the Grand Karate Tournament in Honolulu in 1968, where she met the man she was to leave Elvis for in 1972—International Karate Grand Champion, Mike Stone.

Elvis didn't sour on the sport after this incident. Instead, he incorporated karate into his stage act. In his later appearances, he wore a black mohair *gi*, the karate uniform, and would puncture the air with karate kicks and chops in a dazzling display of virility for the benefit of his audience.

Racquetball

Elvis built a racquetball court at Graceland during the racquetball craze. His court, along with a jacuzzi and a steam room, was housed in a windowless cast-concrete structure in the backyard. When he was at Graceland, Elvis played almost daily.

Football

Elvis called it "the gift from the Gods." He watched the games on TV every Sunday afternoon (his favorite team was the Green Bay Packers). He admired Joe Namath and Johnny Unitas, although he also liked rougher players like Dick Butkus. Elvis called Butkus a "mean mother."

After the game on TV was over, Elvis would go outside and pass around a football in Graceland's backyard. At Elvis' football games, Elvis was always the quarterback, even when Roman Gabriel from the L.A. Rams played. Though the game was just "touch," the pros blocked for real, sometimes leveling Elvis.

The actor Max Baer, Jr., was a regular at the games. Max is best known for the role (which was originally offered to Elvis) of Jethro on "The Beverly Hillbillies." Elvis used to face off against his lookalike, and then slam into him, sending Max flying.

Low-Cal Cuisine

Any dietician will tell you the only real way to bring about and maintain weight loss is to control overeating. Elvis controlled his intake of calories through a specially crafted low-cal cuisine. This diet relies on foods made from Elvis' favorite diet beverage, Diet Shasta soda. Like Proust, who subsisted on

Haaayeeeee.

madeleines and café au lait, Elvis survived for weeks on Diet Shasta gel with bananas.

Shasta Beverages, Inc., is justifiably proud that Diet Shasta has helped many consumers lose weight. To promote this slimming Shasta cuisine, the corporation publishes a recipe booklet, titled "Diet Shasta, 'You Wear It Well.'" The introduction reads:

You know Diet Shasta for its thirteen sparkling flavors. They're tempting, but innocent, with no calories. Old time root beer, bright and bold cola, zippy grapefruit…they all look good on you! Take full advantage of Diet Shasta's flavorful taste by trying some of these exciting recipes. For diet-tired appetites, we've including satisfying, low-cal dessert and beverage ideas. We also give you many of the interesting recipes we've discovered using Diet Shasta in delicious entrees, soups and salads …

The booklet, which Shasta hopes will prove "a valuable addition to your kitchen library," includes recipes for Broiled Filet of Sole with Shasta, Shasta Mushroom Chicken Soup, and Shasta Beef Sukiyaki—all Shasta foods Elvis never really went for. He knew what he liked—Diet Shasta Gel.

Diet Shasta Gel

The cook at Graceland presented Shasta Gel royally for the King. She cut the gel into small bite-sized cubes and built a pyramid out of them: arranging a layer of cubes on a bread plate, she added a slightly narrower second layer, repeating layer after layer until she had formed a cone topped with a single bite-sized piece.

Upon completion, the cook carried the quivering tower of diet gel to Mr. P. When he saw it, he always laughed.

**1 envelope unflavored gelatin
1 12-ounce can Diet Shasta
(Elvis preferred Black Cherry)
1 tablespoon lemon juice
Flavored extract to taste (banana, unless you're using real ones)
Artificial liquid sweetener, to taste
Sliced banana, about 1 cup**

Soften gelatin in ½ cup Diet Shasta. Heat remaining soda to boiling. Add gelatin, stirring until dissolved. Add lemon juice, extract, and sweetener to taste. Chill until set. When basic gel is partially set, fold in sliced bananas.

Yield: **Makes about 1⅔ cups**
Recipe Source: **Shasta Beverage, Inc., diet recipe booklet**

Fluff Topping

For just a few calories more, you can top the gel with this confection.

**⅓ cup chilled Diet Shasta, any fruit flavor
⅓ cup instant nonfat dry milk**

1 tablespoon vanilla extract
1½ tablespoons artificial sweetener
2 or 3 drops almond extract
2 teaspoons lemon juice

Chill mixing bowl, beaters, and diet Shasta. Combine all ingredients in a small deep bowl. Beat at high speed until mixture stands in peaks. Serve on fresh fruit or geletin desert.

Yield: **Makes about 2 cups**
Recipe Source: **Shasta Beverage, Inc., diet recipe booklet**

The Sleeping Beauty Diet

The diet gelatin, the diet pills, the various exercises, even fasting, were all ultimately failures. None of them did the trick. Elvis couldn't keep the weight off. For a while, he considered surgery—a "shunt" or intestinal bypass—where part of his intestine would be removed, but when his doctor told him he would have to adhere to a special diet afterwards, he decided against it. Lamar Fike, Elvis' 300-pound entourage member, had the operation instead. Elvis paid for his beefy friend's bypass. Elvis was so excited that he was not personally having the operation that he celebrated by eating extra cheeseburgers and fries.

Elvis' weight problem was out of control when he appeared in concert swollen to the point that he literally burst out of his pants suit. Something radical had to be done, something that involved no pain, or limits to what he ate. A miracle cure needed to be found.

On a cold winter night in the 1970s, Elvis boarded his plane, the *Lisa Marie*, for a trip to Las Vegas to seek the cure. He was secretly rushed to a doctor's private clinic on a quiet side street. The windows were sealed for privacy. Inside, the doctor and his technicians were ready with dripping hypodermics. Elvis was tucked into a hospital bed. IVs were strapped into his arms. He was about to undertake a miracle cure, a diet which offered no pain and no gain. The cure was "The Sleeping Beauty Diet."

In this diet, the patient literally sleeps his pounds away. Day after day is spent slumbering (actually in a very light coma), until the desired weight is reached. The days consist of blissful dreams without the temptation of fatty foods.

To maintain the coma, barbiturates or narcotics are given orally or by injection. The patient is fed only the most essential nutrients through an IV as the pounds melt away. Obviously, this is a risky diet. Dr. P. G. Auwaerter of Johns Hopkins Hospital warns: "There is no scientific support or substantiation of sleep induction for weight loss. Dangers include toxicity of inducing comatose-like state as well as attendant effects of deep coma, similar to those chronic alcoholics experience. There are also the risks of developing pneumonitis, overdosing, and gagging stomach into lungs."

During Elvis' sleeping beauty diet, he fell out of bed. There was no one in attendance. He was too groggy to get up, but was able to dial one of his friends for help. Elvis was returned to his hospital bed and the diet continued. But after three days, and an unknown number of pounds, Elvis had had enough. During a brief period of consciousness, he asked that the diet be terminated. Elvis never attempted it again.

All of us have our bad days, days when we overeat to the point where self-explosion is imminent. Fortunately, for most of us, these darker days and moods pass. For Elvis, during the last years of his life, though there was always a silver lining, there was always a cloud. Eating, once the source of so much joy in his life, became an addictive and destructive activity.

Like any person with a dependency problem, as Elvis grew more anguished about his condition, he would turn for relief to the dangerous activity which caused so much pain in the first place. Once, when Elvis was about to enter the hospital, he left instructions that he be awakened and fed a cherry pie prior to his departure. He was so nervous about his health that he wolfed down the whole

pie in bed, unaided by the usual utensils.

In his final years, protected by a palace guard at Graceland or Las Vegas, Elvis retreated into his own isolated world. A man who once was so extroverted now enjoyed only solitary pleasures. Food is our earliest pleasure and our first link with our mothers. As life became painful for Elvis, he turned to eating for comfort and companionship. When Elvis ate, he felt safe, as if his mother were still alive, still feeding him, still protecting him.

Elvis' dinners, at the end, instead of marking his collapse into complete decadence, were almost transcendental. "Larger than life" is certainly a misnomer for most celebrities who, in person, are usually distinguishable from ordinary mortals by their rail-thin appearance. Elvis, however, didn't need to diet down to pencil thinness to keep his fans' love. Elvis' fans loved him no matter what size he was—the bigger the better—and Elvis knew this. Elvis attempted to prove that rules of cause and effect that limit the behavior of most humans would not stop him. By eating more than anyone else, Elvis kept earning his title— the King.

Elvis' food intake began careening out of control in the seventies. Even the president seemed to indulge Elvis' behavior. Elvis had arisen one evening in 1970 and decided to disappear from Graceland and fly to Washington to offer his services to President Nixon as an undercover narcotics agent. As part of his "secret mission" Elvis tried to travel incognito, avoiding taking his own plane. He boarded a commercial flight wearing what he thought would be low-profile attire: a crushed velvet purple suit with matching cape. En route, he began to eat compulsively, downing close to

half a pound of chocolates. The stewardesses looked on with concern. Once he arrived in Washington, Elvis headed straight for the White House, but then food cravings got the better of him as he made the cab pull over for a pitstop at a donut shop. Elvis, brandishing a .45 pistol, walked in and ordered a dozen honey donuts. Gobbling them down in the cab Elvis proceeded to the White House gates.

President Nixon agreed to meet him in the Oval Office later in the day. The president presented Elvis with a Bureau of Narcotics and Dangerous Drugs Badge. Elvis sported sunglasses for the ceremony, hiding his bloodshot eyes. His face was badly bloated from his recent binging.

There were numerous similar incidents. Once, while staying in Baltimore prior to a concert, Elvis awakened and ordered a hot fudge sundae for breakfast. He quickly polished it off and ordered a second one. Horrified onlookers could do nothing as they watched Elvis order and eat a third, a fourth, and a fifth sundae for breakfast. Then Elvis passed out.

Though no human could control Elvis' behavior, eventually his own body rebelled. By the time he was forty, it seemed as if Elvis' primary residence was not Graceland, or the Imperial Suite at the Las Vegas Hilton, but a suite at Memphis' Baptist Memorial Hospital.

Elvis in the Hospital

Movie stars and businessmen in the 1950s frequently checked themselves into the hospital just for a "rest." There was absolutely nothing physically wrong with

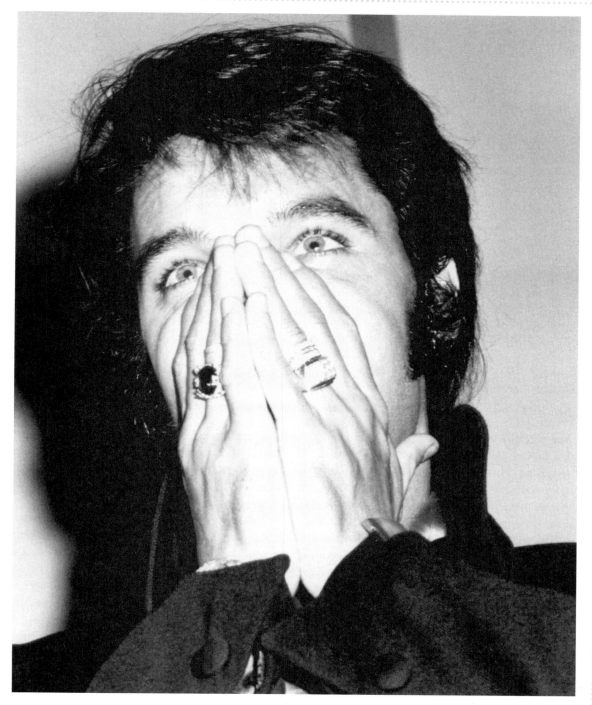

Elvis in his slimmer days.

Mrs. (Nurse) Cocke today on her bike.

them. They were only rich and "exhausted," that is, very rich, and feeling a bit out of sorts, and a stay in the hospital could be a surprisingly hedonistic experience. After a hectic week, there was nothing more relaxing than never having to get out of bed, with full-time nurses in attendance. A private chef retained by the hospital would provide all meals. Doctors Hospital, on New York's Upper East Side, even had a sommelier to assist patients in choosing wines. To enjoy your stay, all you had to have was your money and your health.

Elvis was perhaps the richest man in Memphis and he was constantly hospitalized at Baptist Memorial Hospital. But Elvis wasn't checking in for a "rest"—Elvis was extremely sick. His situation was more severe than just needing to "dry out." Years of overeating and drug abuse had taken their toll. His liver was damaged, his heart enlarged, and his colon twisted.

Patients in Baptist are given a menu order sheet from which they can select their meals. If they are not on a special diet, the patient can choose among a variety of items by circling it. For breakfast, cereal: grits, corn flakes, bran flakes, Rice Krispies, or, the house selection, which is oatmeal. A salad with lunch? The choices are also varied: tossed salad, tomato salad, cole slaw, or congealed fruit salad (the house selection).

People in Memphis say Baptist Memorial Hospital looks just like an opened Bible.

The front is V shaped. Whenever Elvis checked in, the windows of his suite (18ME) were first covered over with tinfoil, to keep out any daylight, as he preferred. Following any medical procedures, it was time to meet with Carol Kidney, the dietitian at Baptist. Ms. Kidney painstakingly went over the day's menu with Elvis, who cooperated with her suggestions. Ms. Kidney went to great lengths to vary his tray, while keeping her eye on his intake. Elvis was not, in fact, on a special diet. His hospital breakfast typically consisted of fresh strawberries, bacon and eggs, toast (which he ate sparingly according to his nurse), and coffee. Lunch and dinner were usually "hamburger steaks," salad, and a vegetable.

After a stay in a hospital, even if only for a "rest" rather than a catastrophic illness, people rarely sit around reminiscing about the food. They don't trade recipes afterwards. Though Elvis appreciated the professionalism of the hospital's dietary staff, hospital cuisine was not something that was immensely pleasurable to Elvis, hence, the recipes will not be presented here.

However, someone at the hospital had a particularly positive impact on Elvis, both on his cuisine and his life. While he was in Baptist Memorial, Elvis grew exceptionally close to his nurse, Marion J. Cocke, the unit supervisor on 18. She was thrilled to have Elvis as a patient. And Elvis was lucky to have Mrs. Cocke as a nurse—she made sure he was comfortable, scheduled various procedures, and ordered his breakfast. Within just a few months they were close personal friends. Elvis gave her a new car, a white Grand Prix. Mrs. Cocke became a frequent visitor to Graceland, and kept a professional eye on what he was eating, up until the very end.

"Sometimes he asked for a bacon burger or hash browns at night, but that certainly was not 'junk food,'" Mrs. Cocke writes in her memoir, *I Called Him Babe: Elvis Presley's Nurse Remembers*. She is unequivocal about Elvis' food preferences, taking the bold but unpopular view that Elvis was in no way addicted to junk food. "At Graceland I never noticed him eating junk food. He was careful about his diet and usually ate balanced meals."

During one of these visits, Elvis asked Mrs. Cocke if she could make banana pudding. Mrs. Cocke replied "sure." The Graceland cooks could make it too, but Elvis wanted Mrs. Cocke's. As soon as she arrived at Graceland the following day, Elvis conspiratorially asked her, "Did you bring it?" She had! She and Elvis put the pudding in the refrigerator. Next Elvis ate an exceptionally light breakfast. Elvis was too guilty to eat dessert without at least the pretense of having tried to eat breakfast first. According to Mrs. Cocke, as the breakfast tray was removed, he held onto the spoon and said, "Now, get the banana pudding!" She did, and Elvis ate it directly out of the bowl in which it was served. He kept spooning it down till he had polished off half the pudding.

Mrs. Cocke, the creator of this exceptional pudding, devotes her life today to charity work. She and her husband, Bob, still live near the hospital. They share their home with their poodle, Aimee, who is blind.

I met with Mrs. Cocke in her immaculate apartment. Unfortunately, our conversation began on the wrong note when I addressed her as Nurse Cocke. She immediately told me she preferred to be called Mrs. Cocke; it sounded strange to her the other way. (Elvis had another nurse at Graceland named Kathy Seamon. This was cause for a lot of merriment for Elvis who cracked jokes that went something like "If Cocke's here, Seamon can't be far behind.")

Mrs. Cocke was quite suspicious of my intentions. She was sure I was just using my questions about banana pudding as a front to glean information about Elvis and drugs. I promised her this wasn't the case. Mrs. Cocke wasn't convinced. She felt she had heard my name before—and she knew where. "The Howard Stern Show." I had been sent by Howard Stern, she insisted. I told her this was absolutely ridiculous. She warned me, "I tape all my interviews." "So do I," I replied.

Soon Mrs. Cocke's suspicions melted away and in their place I discovered the personality that had charmed Elvis so. On her walls were framed pictures of the King. She showed me one which Elvis had autographed, "To Mrs. Cocke, the sex symbol of Babtist!" (Elvis' spelling.) A photo of herself atop a large motorcycle at an Elvis fan club meeting confirmed this other side to Mrs. Cocke.

During her frequent visits to Graceland, Mrs. Cocke would "lather" Elvis' coffee, her term for adding milk and sugar. If he wanted a cool drink after the hot coffee, Mrs. Cocke suggested ice water or "bellywash," which is what she called soda. From then on, Elvis too referred to it as bellywash. Elvis and his nurse were very close indeed.

Mrs. Cocke told me that a few days before he died, Elvis called her and asked her to come to Graceland. It was 3:00 A.M. He had called for her to keep him company. He was lonely. We didn't discuss whether she "lathered" his coffee or poured him bellywash. We discussed what close friends they were and how she comforted him. And how she fed him her soothing banana-cream pudding.

Mrs. Cocke then went into her tidy kitchen and got me the recipe. While she read it out to me, Aimee played on the spic-and-span floors. Mrs. Cocke described herself as a "dump and scratch" baker. Nonetheless, her directions were more precise than any others I encountered on my search for what Elvis ate.

Mrs. Cocke's Banana Pudding

This comforted Elvis more than any other food toward the end of his life.

¾ cup sugar
3 egg yolks
2½ cups milk
¼ cup flour for thickening
1 teaspoon vanilla extract
Vanilla Wafers
Thinly sliced bananas

"Throw in a pot" the sugar, egg yolks, milk, flour, and vanilla extract. Cook till thick over low heat, mixing well. Remove from heat and cool.

In a glass bowl that can be covered, layer some Vanilla Wafers, banana slices, and spoon some of the pudding mixture over top. Repeat the layers until the bowl is full and top with meringue.

Meringue

3 egg whites
3 tablespoons sugar
1 teaspoon vanilla extract

Beats egg whites until stiff. Add the sugar and vanilla. Spoon on top of the pudding and brown in oven. Serve chilled.

Karo Pecan Pie

Mrs. Cocke also gave me the recipe for a second pie she fed Elvis, a healthful pecan pie. What makes her pie so healthful is that it is a recipe for a pecan pie without butter. Clearly, she was keeping an eye on Elvis.

¾ cup sugar
¾ cup white Karo corn syrup
3 eggs
1 teaspoon vanilla
1½ cups pecan halves

Preheat the oven to 375°F. Beat the sugar, Karo, and eggs together real good (Mrs. Cocke suggests using an electric mixer). Add the vanilla and pecan halves. Pour into an unbaked pie crust. Bake at 375°F for 10 minutes. Reduce heat to 325°F until the pie is done in the middle and "quits wiggling," according to Mrs. Cocke.

Elvis' TV Glasses

Despite the best efforts of his nurse and her butterless pecan pie, it was clear that food, the love of Elvis' life, was the love that was destroying him. Elvis went days on end subsisting entirely on ice cream— lots of different flavors swirled together.

Elvis, at the end of his life, became for all intents and purposes bedridden. He increasingly dined while reclining. Though this presented certain eating risks, namely choking, apparently Elvis overcame any difficulties. However, it was impossible to lie flat in bed, eat, and watch the TVs (which were at the foot of the bed) at the same time. Elvis ingeniously thought up the idea of glasses with a mirror inside. The mirror, positioned at a 45-degree angle, reflected the TVs by his feet into his field of vision, which was focused directly upwards.

These tragic dinners alone in bed marked Elvis' final decline. He favored one meal toward the end. It consisted of the foods of his youth: bacon, mashed potatoes, and crowder peas. Sporting his TV glasses, Elvis would swirl the viscous combination together on his plate and then down it in large handfuls. With the TVs at the foot of his bed droning on as his tragic chorus, Elvis ate his way to an early grave.

12 The Last Supper

Elvis never really had one, a last supper. He spent the last days of his life on a nearly complete fast and so never had a proper send-off.

Between 12:30 and 1:00 on the morning of August 16, 1977, Elvis' cook Pauline Nicholson reported to Elvis for work for what was to be the last time. The day cook, Mary, told Pauline that something was wrong with Elvis—he had refused food all day. And Nancy, the cook Mary had relieved, told Mary that Elvis hadn't eaten during her shift either. Pauline was concerned. She made a salad of lettuce, tomatoes, and radishes, and started peeling potatoes. Though she felt Elvis wouldn't eat, she was worried and didn't know what else to do.

Several minutes later, the phone rang in Graceland's

kitchen. It was Mr. P. himself calling her.

"Pauline, would you fix me some water please. Both bottles are empty."

"Sure," said Pauline.

Elvis always liked to have two huge bottles of ice water in the refrigerator next to his bed. For a while, he only drank Mountain Valley Spring Water, but recently he had switched to regular Memphis tap water. Pauline went up to Elvis' room to refill the bottles. She found Elvis lying helplessly ill in bed. She tiptoed around him to pick up one bottle next to his bed and the other in the bathroom. As Elvis looked on from his sickbed, she carried the empty bottles to the icemaker in Lisa Marie's room. Elvis picked up his head to watch her filling the bottles down the hall.

Pauline set down one bottle on the icemaker to start fixing the second. Suddenly, a hand snatched the bottle away. Pauline turned around in fright. It was Elvis. Sick as he was, he had left his bed so that Pauline didn't have to fetch him the water.

"Oh, Mr. P., I'm sorry, why didn't you call? I could have brought your water," said Pauline.

Elvis replied, "Oh, Pauline, that's okay, I needed some exercise anyway."

Pauline watched him depart down the hall, silently carrying the bottle back to his bedroom.

His thirst quenched, Elvis thought about his next move. He had been fasting since finishing a spaghetti dinner a week before for the sole purpose of losing weight for a tour, which was to begin the next evening. After several days of dieting, he still weighed 255 pounds. Discouraged, he gave in. He called the kitchen again, sometime between 2:00 and 4:00 A.M., to break his fast.

He requested what was at that time his favorite snack—ice cream and cookies. This snack typically consisted of at least eight scoops of ice cream and a few dozen cookies. On this night, however, he told Pauline "not to serve as much as usual...just a small amount....And don't give me as many cookies." Pauline took out the ice cream and swirled two flavors together. Going easy, Pauline used less than usual, only four scoops of ice cream and six to eight cookies. She served the ice cream in a cereal bowl accompanied by cookies on a breadplate to the side. Pauline carried it all up to his bedroom where Elvis had not arisen since retrieving the water. She arranged the snack on a tray over him as he lay sprawled on the bed. It was to be his last supper.

The Last Supper

The second flavor of ice cream, after the peach, is unknown. No living person remembers it. Though an autopsy was performed on Elvis, the contents of his stomach were not preserved or examined. Thus the identity of the second flavor of that last meal has been lost to history.

2 scoops of peach, Sealtest
2 scoops of flavor of your choice, Sealtest
6 Chips Ahoy chocolate chip cookies

Mix together the two flavors of ice cream until soft. Serve the cookies on the side. Dip the cookies in the ice cream.

Energy surged through his body. Elvis became ebullient. Radically revitalized by this end to his fast, he discussed the idea of marriage with his girlfriend, Ginger. Using his most affectionate name for her—"Gingerbread"—he told her the wedding would take place when he returned from tour, if possible, in a church shaped like a pyramid.

At 5:00 A.M. Elvis and Ginger went to play racquetball. They were joined at the court behind the mansion by Elvis' cousin Billy Smith, Billy's wife, Jo, and little Lisa Marie. During the day, Elvis had changed into his favorite blue sweatsuit, the one emblazoned with the initials that fascinated him so—DEA—Drug Enforcement Administration.

When Elvis returned to the mansion at nearly 7:00 A.M., he was much more subdued. Pauline encountered him as he made his way up the stairs. Elvis was on the third step when she called to him.

"Mr. P.?"

"Yes, Pauline."

"You look just like somebody hungry to me!"

"You know Pauline, I'm not hungry. I just feel tired. I just want to rest."

Elvis always hugged Pauline goodbye before leaving for a tour. However, that morning, after their exchange, he turned away from her and laboriously continued to climb the stairs. She was never to see him again.

Later in the morning, Elvis called the kitchen again. "Pauline, is Aunt Delta up? If she is up, ask her if she will come

Elvis used to love ice cream.

up here." It was not a request for food. Elvis wanted his "sleeping medication."

Elvis referred to the packet of "sleeping medication" that Aunt Delta was supposed to bring him as his "attack." He typically took three such "attacks" each night, spaced several hours apart. On this last night, he poured out the "little jewels" (as he affectionately called his pills) as usual, but didn't swallow them right away. He waited until he had saved up the contents of all three packets. This last extra large horde comprised (based on coroner's reports) Quaaludes, Valium, Valmid (a hypnotic), Demerol, Amytal, Nembutal, Elavil (antidepressant), Aventyl (antidepressant), codeine, and Sinutab. Elvis took this "sleeping medication," and then drifted off into a slumber from which he would never awaken.

He was found dead several hours later on the floor of his bathroom. Beside him was a favorite book, a gift from his hairdresser, about the Shroud of Turin—*The Scientific Search for the Face of Jesus.*

The official cause of Elvis' death was "cardiac arrythmia" or an uneven heartbeat. The autopsy revealed an enlarged heart, an enlarged colon, narrowing of the arteries, and a fatty liver. This last condition his doctor associated not with fatty food but with his patient's "penchant for eating Tylenol like candy."

The unofficial explanation of Elvis' death focuses on the nonfood substances Elvis ingested that last night: the deadly amount of drugs found in his bloodstream. The intriguing question here is not whether the drugs killed Elvis but whether or not his death was accidental. That is, did Elvis Presley deliberately overdose?

Why did he take all three packets at once that last night? Elvis was usually very careful about the spacing out of his medication. The last night was the only time he ever took all three "attacks" together. David Stanley, Elvis' bodyguard and one of the first to find his body, says "Elvis was too smart to accidentally OD. He knew too much about drugs." For Stanley, Elvis' actions that night point to suicide.

However, if we assume that Elvis was coherent enough to know what he was doing, his taking all three packets at once still doesn't necessarily indicate suicide. Maybe he was being lazy; he couldn't be bothered to wait till it was safe to take the pills. Besides, Elvis hated the idea of suicide. When Freddie Prince committed suicide by shooting himself in the head, Elvis told his stepbrother Billy that Prince had taken the "chickenshit way out."

The more likely explanation of his action is that Elvis took all three packets at once looking for a bigger rush, an effect which would be intensified by his near fast. And it was this fast, plus the paltry "last supper," that offer the real proof that Elvis didn't commit suicide: If Elvis Presley planned to kill himself, would he have spent the last week of his life on a diet?

Epilogue: Elvis Lives?

The Eternal Question

Elvis lives! Maybe Elvis didn't die that fateful August day in 1977, but only faked his death to get some peace and quiet. The body on the floor, the autopsy, and the funeral were perhaps mere props in a cunning ruse to ensure his continued privacy.

Those who maintain that he faked it point to a tape of Elvis supposedly recorded after his death. On it, he explains: "Everything worked just like it was meant to....really needed the rest." Mr. P. says he has spent the time since the fake death on an island: "It's been enjoyable, but it's been a constant battle, growing a beard and this and that, to keep from being recognized."

Unfortunately for those who believe Elvis is still with us, his lifelong dining and drug habits make it unlikely that Elvis could still be alive even if he did fake his death in 1977. Elvis couldn't possibly have lasted much longer; the most extreme high-fiber, low-fat diet wouldn't have saved him. The true miracle is that Elvis even lived to age forty-four.

Nevertheless, flying in the face of logic are the recent sightings of the King, which have a logic all their own. Elvis is always sighted in food-related circumstances—at grocery stores or fast food restaurants.

In 1988 he was spotted in the checkout line at Felpausch's grocery in Vicksburg, Michigan, sporting an all-white jumpsuit and a motorcycle helmet. At the same time, there were reports that he was living in nearby Kalamazoo, Michigan, at the Columbia Plaza Hotel. He supposedly registered under the name John Burrows. Whenever the curious tried to reach "John" they were told he was out to lunch at Wendy's, on East Michigan Avenue.

The most convincing sighting of all is that by Louise Welling, a Michigan housewife. Louise saw Elvis in 1988 at the Kalamazoo Burger King on South Westnedge Avenue. Elvis was in a red Ferrari and was ordering a Whopper at the drive-through window. What gives Louise's account an eerie credibility is that although Louise couldn't possible have known it, Burger King was by far Elvis' favorite fast food chain (perhaps something about the name reminded him of himself).

Could it be that the man spotted eating around town was just an Elvis impersonator, grabbing lunch? The eyewitnesses swear it was no impersonator: It was Elvis himself. If Elvis is dead, then who is this mysterious Elvis, spotted at Burger King years after his own death? It could be Elvis' ghost. Ghosts don't eat; Elvis, though spotted after his death in checkout lines and at Burger King, has never actually been seen eating. And it does make perfect sense that a ghostly specter of Elvis would still choose to roam through supermarkets, Wendy's, or Burger Kings—all his favorite haunts in life.

Elvis' death was tragic for his fans but it was most devastating to his family. Priscilla and Lisa Marie turned from Elvis cuisine after the death of the King, to the fancier foods served by Priscilla's then-boyfriend, the supermodel Michael Edwards. Edwards, in his own words "a bronze-sculpted Greek god, exuding virility, eyes burning passionately, long hair wild and flowing," was a passionate gourmet. According to Edwards, his enormous collection of "professional cookware hanging over the stove" made a deep impression on Priscilla during her first visit to his apartment. Edwards secured her affection when he told her, "You've never experienced haute cuisine until you've tried mine."

Priscilla once told Andy Warhol that she never ate caviar because Elvis never let her. She was readily seduced by Edwards' culinary offerings. She dined night after night with her new boyfriend on gourmet foods accompanied by rare wines. The suave male model, a native of Pensacola, Florida, was shocked by Priscilla's table manners. He claims Priscilla stacked dirty plates on the table after they finished each course. The waiters looked on, horrified. "Baby, you don't have to clear the table," he told her after one embarrassing incident in the Polo Lounge of the Beverly Hills Hotel. Priscilla explained why she did: "I always did it for Elvis. He didn't like dirty dishes in front of him, ever."

Once Priscilla was suitably trained to Edwards' standards, he moved into her Beverly Hills mansion. Edwards celebrated by cooking her a special gourmet dish that night, fish "Barcelona style."

Michael Edwards' Fish Barcelona-Style

To make fish Barcelona à la Michael Edwards gut the the fish but leave the head on. Edwards cannot overemphasize the importance of the head to his recipe. In his memoir, *Priscilla, Elvis, and Me*, he writes about the fish:

*I decided to surprise Priscilla...
I started preparing a whole fish and Priscilla exclaimed, "Aren't you going to cut the head off?"
"No, all its juice would leak out."
Holding up the fish and wiggling it at her, I said, "We wouldn't want that, would we?"
She blushed and said, "Michael, you're terrible."
"It's true," I said. "All the best juices are in the head."*

Keeping this in mind, you are now ready to begin the recipe itself. All directions are Michael Edwards'.

6 large shrimp
1 whole cleaned and gutted fish
1 garlic clove, peeled
1 tomato, chopped
1 onion, chopped
2 boiled potatoes
Olive oil
1 glass white wine
Bouquet of herbs

Preheat oven to 375° F. Devein six large shrimp and stuff them inside the cleaned fish; place fish in a baking dish. Add the garlic, tomato, onion, and potatoes to the baking dish, placing them around the fish. Sprinkle olive oil lightly over all, and then empty your wine glass into it. Take every herb in your spice cabinet, pour some of each in the palm of your hand, and, rubbing your hands together vigorously, let it rain on the fish. Never sprinkle herbs direct from the container; they have to be ground in your hand to bring out the full bouquet. Cover and bake. By the time you finish having a quickie, about 45 minutes later, the fish will be ready to eat and so will you.

Note to the reader: **Edwards doesn't specify what wine he was sipping before his quickie, but any cooking wine will do.**

For Edwards and Priscilla, though the relationship was not to last, the fish was a success. Edwards reports that he and Priscilla devoured their candlelit "nuptial feast" by the pool. Edwards wrote, "I felt the first stirrings of love for her that evening."

Each Elvis fan remains close to Elvis in his or her own way. Lela Avon is one of his fans who thinks Elvis is still alive. She is excited though not surprised by all the sightings at Burger Kings. It is unthinkable to her that he is dead. She knows he is alive. Like many Elvis fans, she wants to spot Elvis herself. Unlike anybody else, Lela thinks she has found a way to contact him.

Miss Avon is a reclusive 350-plus pound resident of New York City's East Village, a neighborhood of hustlers, aging hipsters, urchins, and people just down on their luck like herself. The hefty twenty-four-year old (she looks a decade older) originally came to New York hoping to break into film or the "music biz." But when she got "big," Lela stopped looking for work. She survives on disability checks. Lela doesn't go out much now. Her favorite non-Elvis reading material is *We Deliver*, a guide to Manhattan restaurants' takeout menus.

Behind the triple-locked doors of her third-floor tenement studio, the decrepit New York streets give way to Elvis World. Lela's walls are completely covered with colorful pictures of Elvis— vacationing in Hawaii, strutting on a Vegas stage, relaxing at Graceland. Elvis' music is always playing. A life-size portrait of Elvis on black velvet hangs above her bed. Elvis' birthday is more important to Lela than her own.

Twice a year, Lela makes a special corn bread. The smell of baking bread and cornmeal fills the small apartment, and Lela hums Elvis hymns to herself while she mixes the ingredients. There is flour all over the kitchenette. As Lela lovingly kneads the dough with her large hands, you might guess that Lela is from the Deep South and that the recipe is a family heirloom. But Lela isn't from the South; she is from the Laguna Hills area in Los Angeles. And when asked where she got the recipe, her little red eyes became fiery under her uneven brown bangs, and she hisses, "from the spirits."

Lela isn't mixing dough for normal corn bread. Lela is making chocolate corn bread. The spirits have told her to do this. She is making it for Elvis. The spirits have told her that the chocolate corn bread, a combination unknown to Elvis, will lure him back.

The two times a year she makes it, on Elvis' birthday and the day he "died," she sets the warm bread with its chocolate coating on her windowsill. Through the open window the enticing smell drifts out over Avenue A. Lela is always hopeful the lure will work; it's like setting out food for the Easter Bunny or Elijah or Santa. Any knock on the door could be Elvis. (Lela says she will just feel it beforehand when it's the real thing.) The corn bread hasn't lured the King yet. At the end of the day, Lela shuts the window and eats the chocolate corn bread herself.

Lela has a mission. Her life and her corn bread have so far been a failure, even by her own standards. However, when Miss Avon describes her mission, she becomes uncharacteristically excited, and rightly so. With pressured speech she describes her hopes: "If everyone made this special corn bread for Elvis on the same day all across America, everyone baking this recipe in their own kitchen, the collective spirit would bring about a miracle. Yes, a miracle. Somewhere, wherever Elvis is, Elvis will be unable to resist this national offering. The smell of freshly baked chocolate corn bread will blanket the country and smoke him out. There will be that knock at the kitchen door, at a house in some little town or maybe right here at my kitchen in New York. And when the door was opened, standing there will be Elvis."

To further this miracle, Lela has generously shared her recipe for chocolate corn bread. She insists on pointing out that it isn't really her recipe. It comes from beyond.

Chocolate Corn Bread (From the Spirits) for Elvis

1 box Jiffy Cornbread Mix
1 can Hershey's Chocolate Syrup

Preheat oven to 350° F. Grease a 9-by 9-inch pan. Prepare the cornbread according to directions on box. Combine half a can Hershey's syrup into the batter and bake for 15 to 17 minutes, or until tester inserted in middle of bread comes out clean. Pour remaining syrup over hot cake and serve warm.

Photography Credits

Index

Page numbers in italic refer to illustrations.

A

Aladdin Hotel and Casino, Las Vegas, *100*, 124–25, 128, 129, 131
Anders, Dr., 44, 45
apple pie, 54–55
army food
    Christmas dinner, 60
    cooking tips, 51
    cook school, 9, *42*, 43–47, *46*, *47*
    in Elvis' day, 48, 49–50, 55–56, 57–58, 60–62
    garrison, 45
    quality of, 48–49
    rations, 45, 61–62
    recipes for, 51–55
    standardized menu, 49, 57–58
Ausborn, James, 21
Auwaerter, P.G., 137

B

Babcock, Martha, 40–41
baby food, 16, 17
bacon, 18, 75
    Fool's Gold Loaf, 97–99
Baer, Max, Jr., 135
banana
    and peanut butter sandwich, fried, 41, 73, 99
    pudding, 86–87
    pudding, Mrs. Cocke's, 143, 144
Baptist Memorial Hospital, Memphis, 140, 142–43
barbecued pork chops, 83
barbecue pizza, Coletta's, *95*, 95, 96–97
bean soup, navy, of the U.S. Army, 52
beef
    chicken fried steak (ugly steak), 66, 67, 68–69, 77
    corned beef hash, 58
    creamed chipped on toast (Shit on a Shingle), 45, 62, 63
    hamburger, 84
    hamburger, Palm Beach burger, 38
    meat loaf, 54, 81–82
    roast, 81
    sloppy joes, 31
    steak Diane, 129
beverages
    alcohol, 102, 104–5
    buttermilk, 82
    chocolate shake à la Gridiron, 38, 39
    Coca-Cola float, 39
    coffee, 55, 82
    Diet Shasta, 135–36, *136*
    iced tea, 18, 83
    lemonade, 55
    Pepsi, 72, 98
birthday cake, 105
biscuits, buttermilk, 76
black-eyed peas, 86
Blackwood Brothers, 35
Blue Hawaii, 118, 121
breads, quick
    biscuits, buttermilk, 76
    spoon bread, cheese, 31
    See also corn bread
breakfast
    in army, 48, 49, 58
    at Graceland, 67, 72, 74–76, 102
    Grandma's food, 58–59
    on Hollywood set, 115
    in hospital, 142
    in Las Vegas, 102
    in Paris, 62
brown betty, 54
Brown, Helen Gurley, 99
Burger King, Elvis sightings at, 151–52
burritos, 107
butter cookies, 30, 46, 47
buttermilk, 82
    biscuits, 76

C

cake(s)
    birthday, 105
    caramel, 87–88
    pineapple, 88
    wedding, 131
Campbell, Bill, 114
candy snack, 37
caramel cake, 87–88
Carter, June, 35
celebrity cuisine, 113
cereal
    cold, 75
    oatmeal, 75
Chasen, Dave, 111
cheese
    and grits, 19
    and peanut butter sandwich, 94
    spoon bread, 31
Chesnut, Nessie, 15
chess pie, 23
chicken, oven-fried, with potato chips, 22
chicken fried steak (ugly steak), 66, 67, 68–69, 77
chocolate shake à la Gridiron, 38, 39
Christmas dinner, army, 60
Christy, George, 110–13, *111*
church picnics ("dinner on the ground"), 9, *20*, 21, 22, 23
Clambake, 121
Coca-Cola float, 39
Cocke, Marion J., *142*, 143–44
coffee, 18, 55, 82, 144
Coletta's Italian Restaurant, barbecue pizza of, *95*, 95–97
collard greens, 16
Colorado Gold Mine Company, Denver, 97, 98
cookies
    butter, 30, 46, 47
    grape-nut flakes, Memphis schools', 29
corn bread, 80
    chocolate, 153–54
    goody mush, 16
    Miss Vertie's, 15
    soaks, 17
corn cakes, 80
corned beef hash, 58
crepes Suzette, 129
crowder peas, 68, 79
Curtiz, Michael, 116

D

Datz, Jeanne, 119
death bed food, 144, 145, 148, *149*
diet food, 104, 105, 116, 135–37

diet pills, 134
dill pickles, 93
    fried, 36
dip, lemon-anchovy, Barbara Eden's, 118
doughnuts, Krispy Kreme, 93–94, 94
Down, Lora, 153–54
dressing, oyster, with turkey, 61
Dr. Strangelove, 37
Dudie's Diner, Tupelo, 21
Dundee, Elaine, 13

E

Eden, Barbara, 9, 110, *114,* 114–18
Edwards, Michael, 152–53
eggs
    Elvis style, 74
    omelet, 51, 102
Elvis cuisine
    baby foods, 16, 17
    at church picnics ("dinner on the ground"), 9, *20,* 21, 22, 23
    at concerts, 106
    death bed, 143, 144, 145, 148, *149*
    diet, 104, 105, 116, 135–37, 145
    Grandma's food, 58–59
    in Hollywood restaurants, 110–13
    on Hollywood set, 113–17, *115*
    in hospital, 142, 143
    Italian food, 28, 29, 95–96, 112
    in Las Vegas, 102, *122,* 123–25, 127–29, *128*
    Mom's food, 13, 17, 18–19, 41
    in movies, 121
    Polynesian food, 118–20
    popular origins of, 8–9
    on road trips, 70, 83–85, 102–3,106–7
    in roadside restaurants, 21, *34,* 36, 37–40, 103
    in school cafeteria, *24,* 25, 26,*27,* 27–31, *30*
    in sex life, 9, 99, 107, 121
    snack food, 37, 41, 91–99, 103
    Southern, 13, 103–4
    teen culture and, 33–34
    wedding, 131
    See also army food; Graceland food; *specific recipes*
Esposito, Joe, 67

F

Fike, Lamar, 137
First Assembly of God (Holy Rollers),19
Fischer, David Hackett, 13
fish, Barcelona-style, Michael Edwards', 152–53
Fisher, M. F. K., 99
Flaming Star, 114
fluff topping, 136–37
Fool's Gold Loaf, 97–99
football, 29, 135
Four Flames restaurant, Memphis, 37
fruit cocktail salad, 82

G

Gel, Diet Shasta, 136–37
Girls! Girls! Girls!, 121
Goldman, Albert, 109
goody mush, 16
Graceland, *64*
    closed–circuit video system at, 69,73–74
    dining room at, 72
    garden at, 79
    jungle room at, 72, 97, 118
    kitchen at, 67, 72, 105
    sports at, 134–35
Graceland food
    beverages, 82–83
    breakfast, 67, 72, 74–76, 102
    cooks of, *65,* 65–69, *66,* 72, 107
    desserts, 86–89
    dinner, 67–69, 77–81, 103, 104
    at dinner parties, 73, 81–83
    New Year's, 85–86, 104–5
    shopping list, 69–72
    tips on preparation, 73–75
grape-nut flakes cookies, Memphis schools', 29
gravy, 78
    onion, 78
green beans, 68
    fresh, 79
greens, 79–80
    Miss Vertie's, 16
Gridiron Restaurant, Memphis, *34,* 37–40
grits, 18
    and cheese, 19
    hominy, fried, 52

H

ham, 85
    baked, with raisin sauce, 53
hamburgers, 84
    Palm Beach burger, 38
    roadside food, 21, 38, 92, 103, 113
    from room service, 127–28
    sausage burgers, 84
Harrison, Ann, 44, 45, 46
Hawaii, Polynesian food of, 118–20
Hilton Hawaiian Village Hotel, 119
Hine, Thomas, 34
Hollywood restaurants, 110–13
Hollywood roadhouse, Memphis, 36
hominy grits, fried, 52
hotcakes, 51–52
hot dog roll snack, 93, 103
Humes High School, Memphis, 26–29

I

ice cream
    binge eating, 140
    chocolate shake à la Gridiron, 38, 39
    Coca-Cola float, 39
    as death bed food, 145, 148, 149
iced tea, 18, 83
icing, 87–88, 131
intestinal bypass surgery, 137
Italian food, 28, 29, 112

K

karate, 134, 135
Kennedy, Jerry, 97
ketchup, 67–68
Kidney, Carol, 143
King Creole, 116
Klein, George, 95
Krispy Kreme doughnuts, 93–94, 94

L

Lacker, Marty, 70
Las Vegas food, 102, *122,* 123–25, 127–29, *128*
Las Vegas Hilton (International), 126–28, *127, 128*
lemonade, 55
Lennon, John, 63

Liberty Land Amusement Park, 36
Lillian, Aunt, 13, 14, 19
Love Me Tender, 72, 113
Lyon, Ann, 40

M

McAleer, Mac, 94
Madeo restaurant, Los Angeles, 110–12
Mansfield, Elisabeth, 58, 59
Mansfield, Rex, 56, 134
meat loaf, 54, 81–82
Memphian Theater, 36–37
Memphis, Tennessee
    Baptist Memorial Hospital in,
        140,142–43
    restaurants in, 37–39, 95–96, 103
    school cafeteria food in, *24,* 25,26,
        27, 27–31, *30*
Mississippi Slim, 14, 21
mustard greens, 16

N

navy bean soup of the U.S. Army, 52
Naylor, Tiny, 113
Newman, Paul, 111
New Year's cuisine, 85–86, 104–5
Nicholson, Pauline, *65,* 65–69, *66,* 74,76,
    77, 78, 81–82, 83, 86, 87,147–48,
    149
1950s food, 34–35
Nixon, Richard, 97, 140

O

oatmeal, 75
omelet, 51, 102
onion gravy, 78
oyster dressing, with turkey, 61
Ozuna, Bobbie Joe, 128

P

Palm Beach burger, 38
pancakes
    crepes Suzette, 129
    hotcakes, 51–52
    taro-potato, with grilled Molokai

venison sausage, 120
Parker, Colonel, 103, 113–14, 126, 131
Party, The, 37
Pascagoula, Mississippi, 21
peanut butter
    and banana sandwich, fried, 41, 73,99
    and cheese sandwich, 94
    on crackers, 17
    Fool's Gold Loaf, 97–99
peas
    black-eyed, 86
    crowder, 68, 79
pecan pie, Karo, 145
pepper sauce, hot enough to send a UFO
    flying, 16
Pepsi, 72, 98
pickles. *See* dill pickles
pie(s)
    apple, 54–55
    chess, 23
    crust, 54–55, 89
    pecan, Karo, 145
    sweet potato, 88
Pietrafeso, Ron, 97
pineapple cake, 88
pizza, barbecue, Coletta's, *95,* 95, 96–97
plating, 99
poke salad, 104
Polynesian food, 118–20
popsicles, 92
pork
    barbecue pizza, Coletta's, *95,* 95,
        96–97
    chops, 18
    chops, barbecued, 83
    See also bacon; ham; sausage
potato(es)
    fried, sandwich, 59, 60
    fries, 85
    mashed, 68, 78
    –taro pancakes, with grilled
        Molokai venison sausage, 120
Prell, Milton, 131
Presley, Dee (stepmother), 101
Presley, Elvis, *10, 32, 76, 90, 108,141*
    alcohol consumption of, 102, 104–5
    with army abroad, 57–63, 63
    army induction and training, 47–48,
        49, 56
    Audubon Drive home of, 40–41, 72
    birth of, 11–12
    Cadillac of, 35–36
    childhood of, 14–15, 17–19, 21
    church of, 19, 21

death of, 145, 147–50
death of mother, 57
dressing style of, 27, 112, 127
drug use by, 106, 134, 150
eating binges of, 139–40
eating habits of, 72, 101–7
entertaining by, 36–37, 73, 97–98
Graceland home of. *See* Graceland
hairstyle of, 27
in Hawaii, 118, 119
health problems of, 142
in high school, 26–28
high school prom of, 35
Hollywood dates of, 113
hospitalization of, 140, 142–43
jet plane of, 97–98, 137
jobs of, 28, 35
in Las Vegas, 102, *124,* 125, *126,*
    126–28, *138, 146*
meeting with Priscilla, 62
meteoric rise of, 14, 35
movie favorites of, 37
movies of, 72, 109–10, *112,* 113,
    114, 116, 117, 118, 121
nocturnal habits of, 65, 77, 92–93
in Paris, 62
populuxe era of, 34–35
poverty of family, 19, 28
reasons for overeating, 106, 107,140
relationship with mother, 19, 40,
    41, 56–57
sightings of, 151–52, 153
sports and exercise, 29, *132,* 134–35,
    135
television watching, 72, 106, 117,135,
    145
wedding to Priscilla, 125, *130,* 131
weight gain of, 105, 115, 116, 127,
    133, 137.
weight loss techniques of, 116,
    133–37, 148
    See also Elvis cuisine
Presley, Gladys (mother), *10*
    birth of twins to, 11–12
    childhood poverty of, 14
    church of, 19, 21
    cooking style/specialties,
        13, 17, 18–19, 41
    culinary inspiration for, 14, 15
    death of, 57, 105
    relationship with Elvis, 19, 40, 41,
        56–57
Presley, Jessie (brother), 12
Presley, Lisa Marie (daughter), 149, 152

Presley, Priscilla Beaulieu (wife), 62, *124*
 at Graceland, 67, 81, 83, 95, 96
 and karate, 134
 relationship with Michael Edwards, 152, 153
 wedding of, 125, *130,* 131
Presley, Vernon (father), 11, 12, 21, 26, 27, 41, 57
 in Germany, 58, 60
 in prison, 18, 19
 remarriage of, 101
Presley, Vester (uncle), 17
Prince, Freddie, 150
pudding, banana, 86
 Mrs. Cocke's, 143, 144

Quigley, Vertice "Miss Vertie," 12, *14,* 14–15, 17

racquetball, 134
raisin sauce, with baked ham, 53
rations, 45, 61–62
Rendezvous restaurant, Memphis, 103
restaurants
 Hollywood, 110–13
 Italian, 95–97, 112
 Las Vegas, *122,* 123–25
 roadside, 21, *34,* 36, 37–40, 103
roast beef, 81

salad, 82
 fruit cocktail, 82
 7-up, 23
sandwich(es)
 Fool's Gold Loaf, 97–99
 fried potato, 59, 60
 peanut butter and banana, fried, 41, 73, 99
 peanut butter and cheese, 94

sloppy joes, 31
sauce
 pepper, hot enough to send a UFO flying, 16
 raisin, with baked ham, 53
 See also gravy
sausage, 75
 burgers, 84
 Molokai venison, grilled, with taro-potato pancakes, 120
school cafeteria food, *24,* 25, 26, *27,* 27–31, *30*
Seamon, Kathy, 144
Sellers, Peter, 37
7-up salad, 23
Shasta, Diet, 135–36, *136*
 Gel, 136–37
Shit on a Shingle, 45, 62, 63
shrimp, 105
 Island Mahi Mahi and Kahuku, brochette of, 120
sleep induction for weight loss, 137
sloppy joes, 31
Smith, Billy and Jo, 149
snack food, 37, 41, 91–99, 103
snow cream, 92
soaks, 16, 17, 58–59
soup, navy bean, of the U.S. Army, 52
Southern food tradition
 Appalachian *vs* coastal, 13
 in army, 45
 Elvis' family and, 15–18, 103–4
spam, 55–56
spoon bread, cheese, 31
squirrel, fried, 17
Stanley, Billy, 8, 37, 92, 101–7, *102,* 128, 133, 150
Stanley, David, 150
steak
 chicken fried, 66, 67, 68–69, 77
 Diane, 129
Stern, Jane and Michael, 118
Stone, Mike, 134
sweet potato(es)
 candied, 86
 pie, 88–89

Tate, Corinne, 18
Thompson, Linda, 92
tomatoes, fried green, 18
Tupelo, Mississippi, 11–13, 21
turkey, with oyster dressing, 61
Turner, Roy, 13
turnip greens, 16

U.S. Army Cook School, Fort Lee, 9, *42,* 43–47, *46, 47*

Vaughn, Regis, 35
vegetables, 13
 Molokai, terrine of, wrapped in Nori, 119
 See also names of vegetables
venison sausage, Molokai, grilled, with taro-potato pancakes, 120

Wagner, Robert, *115*
Watkins, Shirley, *28,* 29
wedding cake, 131
Welling, Louise, 151–52
Wentzell, Lloyd, 124–25
West, Red, 29, 35, 59
Williams, Esther, 62
Wood, Anita, 56
Wood, Natalie, 113

yams, candied, 86
Yancey, Becky, 36
yogurt, 92